PAGAN PORTALS – HERBS OF THE SUN, MOON AND PLANTS

The spirit here might at fii   )tain
Beefheart or Dr William Pri   but
read and you'll find a work   ..ci ɔalist
ground breaker of considera.   _ϲυμe. Steve Andrews, poet, mystic, and author of distinction rides again.
Peter Finch

As the Keeper of the Stones here at Avebury, the knowledge of the herbs, plants and trees is a daily wonder, and this knowledge is there in this intriguing book, for all to unlock the secrets of their magic and uses. A beneficial "right" arm to those full of questions! Seek the knowledge and you will understand – highly recommended!
Terry Dobney (Archdruid of Avebury and Keeper of the Stones)

Another fascinating piece of writing by Steven Andrews, *Herbs of the Sun, Moon and Planets* contains a wealth of material which will be of interest, not only to naturalists and astrologers, but to students of folklore, of the history of ideas, and the general public too. Easy to read, cram-packed with information and an insight into the minds of our naturalist forefathers, every paragraph offers a new thought to ponder on. Buy this book. You won't be disappointed.
C.J. Stone

Steve has put together a useful little reference book for some of the wonderful planetary herbs and plants with history, myths and medicinal uses, an interesting read.
Rachel Patterson

Steve's first book *Herbs of the Northern Shaman* has been an invaluable companion for the Practical Pagan Magickal Herb classes I offer in my adopted home of Ibiza, Spain. As a practising White Witch, Firewalker and Faery Goddess, I was delighted to hear that Steve is now offering a second volume, and this too, is chock full of information and herb lore. So perfect for our Elemental ceremonies here on the magickal Isle of Tanit. Thank you Steve! Blessed Be!

Carli Susu, White Witch

Pagan Portals

Herbs of the Sun, Moon and Planets

Pagan Portals

Herbs of the Sun,
Moon and Planets

Steve Andrews

Winchester, UK
Washington, USA

First published by Moon Books, 2016
Moon Books is an imprint of John Hunt Publishing Ltd., Laurel House, Station Approach,
Alresford, Hants, SO24 9JH, UK
office1@jhpbooks.net
www.johnhuntpublishing.com
www.moon-books.net

For distributor details and how to order please visit the 'Ordering' section on our website.

Text copyright: Steve Andrews 2015
Illustrations copyright: judithfhubbard

ISBN: 978 1 78535 302 4
Library of Congress Control Number: 2015952168

A CIP catalogue record for this book is available from the British Library.

Design: Lee Nash

Printed and bound by CPI Group (UK) Ltd, Croydon, CR0 4YY, UK

We operate a distinctive and ethical publishing philosophy in all
areas of our business, from our global network of authors to
production and worldwide distribution.

CONTENTS

To Melissa

Introduction

This book is about the herbs of other planets in the solar system, so is certainly a bit different from many other herbals. But how can there be herbs on the other planets you are no doubt asking? Well, the answer is simple: the plants don't grow on other worlds, but are ruled over by planetary deities, each of which has its own special characteristics and associations.

The historic herbalists, such as Nicholas Culpeper, came up with ways of grouping herbs into various categories so that they had a reference guide to their properties and knew which ones to try using to treat specific ailments.

For example, there was the means of classification known as the Doctrine of Signatures, whereby a plant was named after a part of the body it was thought to resemble and then believed to be a good remedy for illnesses affecting that area. Lungwort (*Pulmonaria officinalis*), with its broad and spotted leaves, was thought to have a similarity to the human lungs, and so this herb was thought to be good for respiratory complaints. The Doctrine of Signatures was one method ancient herbalists used, but there was another, because they also decided that, just as in astrology it is believed that specific planets and their gods rule over individual zodiac signs, the same principle applied to herbs.

Mars is known as the god of war and so all plants he ruled over had some sort of Martian characteristic. They might have red berries or red sap, or perhaps their juice was caustic. They might be covered in spines or able to sting. In other words they had something about them that was warlike and aggressive.

By contrast, the Roman goddess Venus was associated with love, beauty, sexuality and growth. The dainty herb known as Vervain (*Verbena officinalis*) is a herb of Venus, and in witchcraft it is used in rituals and spells to attract love.

Sometimes it isn't so obvious as to why a herb has been

chosen to have a particular planetary ruler, but usually there are characteristics we can see and understand as to why the herbalists agreed that a plant was ruled by a specific deity.

Herbalism according to the planetary rulers of the plants and spices makes a fascinating study and could perhaps inspire some interesting herb garden collections. It would be possible to collect and grow species that represent each planet, with herbs of the Sun growing in a circle in the middle of the garden. Yes, there are herbs that are thought to be ruled by the Sun as well, and also by the Moon. These two very important heavenly bodies are included in this work as well with some of the plants they have dominion over, and both are thought of as 'planets' from the point of view of practitioners of the esoteric and occult arts. I have decided to choose seven herbs for each planetary ruler.

Of course, not all herbalists, ancient or modern, agreed on everything, and so there are some herbs that are listed under more than one planet. They may well have characteristics that could represent either and thus the confusion. Others are so obvious that once you get to understand the rules behind this you can often spot what planet rules a specific herb just by looking at the plant. It will certainly give you plenty to think about!

Herbs of the Sun

Sunflower
helianthus

The Sun is at the centre of the solar system in which our planet is also located and gives light to all the planets it can reach. It has long been worshipped and thought of as the source of all life and as Father Sun. It is the light-giver that with its rays illuminates all it shines on. Without it, life could not survive. Its keywords are power, vitality and self-expression.

Chamomile *(Anthemis nobilis/Chamaemelum nobile)*

Chamomile is a herb of the Sun that besides liking to grow in sunny places has white petals that surround its yellow centre and can be likened to the Sun's rays. It is an aromatic perennial plant with a creeping habit and finely-cut feathery leaves. Chamomile comes from Europe, but is widely distributed in North America and grown in herb gardens in many parts of the world.

It has a long history of usage both as a medicinal herb and for cosmetic purposes. William Turner, in his *Newe Herball* (1551), declared: 'Thys herbe was consecrated by the wyse men of Egypt unto the Sonne and was rekened to be the only remedy for all agues.' According to Mrs M. Grieve in her *A Modern Herbal*: 'The old herbals agree that 'it is but lost time and labour to describe it.'' It was known in times gone by as the 'Plant's Physician'.

The Ancient Greeks called it 'Earth Apple', and its generic name is derived from *kamai,* which means 'on the ground' and *melon,* meaning Apple. Indeed, the herb has an Apple-like aroma when lightly crushed.

The Anglo Saxons knew Chamomile as 'Maythen' and it was one of the sacred herbs of Woden. According to the *Lacnunga*, in the Harleian manuscript collection of the British Museum, it was included in the Nine Herbs Lay, a charm against the effects of 'lying venom' and 'loathed things that over land rove'.

In herbal medicine Chamomile is used for its soothing and sedative properties. Taken as a herb tea it is good for indigestion, nausea, to promote a good night's sleep and is helpful for painful menstruation. Ointments made with Chamomile are used to treat skin complaints such as eczema. As a steam inhalation, the herb is regarded as a remedy for sinusitis and asthma. The dried flowers are added to herbal pillows to help fight insomnia and also included in pot-pourri. An infusion of the flowers is used to help lighten blonde hair and as a skin freshener. The whole Chamomile herb can be used to make a herbal beer.

The herbalist Parkinson wrote in his *Earthly Paradise* (1656):

Camomil is put to divers and sundrey users, both for pleasure and profit, both for the sick and the sound, in bathing to comfort and strengthen the sound and to ease pains in the diseased.

Chamomile lawns are popular in ornamental gardens because of their fragrance. The plant is often included in herb gardens too.

Eyebright *(Euphrasia officinalis)*
Eyebright is a herb of the Sun that, as its name suggests, is recom-

mended for treating the eyes. Its tiny white flowers have a yellow centre with darker purple ray markings and perhaps this is why it was associated with the Sun. It was the Doctrine of Signatures though that saw a likeness between this herb and the organ used for sight. It was thought that the markings in the flower resembled a bloodshot eye.

Its scientific name *Euphrasia* means 'gladness' and this is thought to have been bestowed upon this herb because of the joy felt if an eyesight problem was cured by its use. Hildegard of Bingen in her *Physica*, compiled circa 1150, recommended it as a herb to treat eye complaints. Fuchs and Dodoens did likewise in the 16th century when they also listed it as a herb to treat eye problems with.

Eyebright was known to the poets Spenser and Milton as the Euphrasy. Milton wrote that the Archangel Michael used it when ministering to Adam after the Fall: '...to nobler sights Michael from Adam's eyes the film removed, Then purged with euphrasine and rue, His visual orbs for he had much to see.'

Eyebright is an annual semi-parasitic herb found growing in grassland and grassy places on heaths and in sand dunes. It has a liking for poor soils and attaches itself to the roots of grasses, from which it then absorbs nutrients. If it is transplanted into a garden it will only grow if surrounded by grass. Eyebright is found in many parts of the UK, Europe, Siberia and the Himalayas.

Eyebright is gathered in full flower in July and August. The whole plant is dried and used to make infusions that are used to treat sore and itchy eyes as eyewash. The herb is used the same way as a remedy for conjunctivitis. It has definite anti-inflammatory properties and this makes it useful for treating hayfever, rhinitis, sinusitis and catarrh. It is taken as a weak infusion three to four times daily for these ailments and also for jaundice and abdominal spasms. Eyebright is an ingredient in British Herbal Tobacco, which has been smoked as a remedy for bronchial infections.

In Iceland Eyebright has also been used a treatment for the eyes, and the Highlanders of Scotland made an infusion of the herb in milk, which was then applied to inflamed eyes with the use of a feather that was dipped into the liquid.

Culpeper gave details of an eye lotion containing the herb:

An Excellent Water to Clear the Sight.
Take of Fennel, Eyebright, Roses, white, Celandine, Vervain and Rue, of each a handful, the liver of a Goat chopt small, infuse them well in Eyebright Water, then distil them in an alembic, and you shall have a water will clear the sight beyond comparison.

Juniper (*Juniperus communis*)

The Juniper is an evergreen small tree with reddish bark and is a herb of the Sun. It has spiky needles and male and female flowers on separate plants. The female ones are in the form of small green cones that eventually ripen after as long as two or three years into blue-black 'berries'. The Juniper comes from Europe, Scandinavia, North America and Asia and grows on mountains, heaths and scrubland with poor and chalky soils. It is also frequently grown in parks and gardens for its ornamental value.

The ancient Egyptians are said to have used Juniper in the process of the embalming of their dead and also for magical and medicinal purposes. Juniper incense is believed to repel evil and to help purify the air as well as driving away disease. Since Biblical times it has been seen as a herb of protection. 'Elijah went a day's journey into the wilderness and came and sat down under a Juniper tree.' (1 Kings 19:4) It is associated with justice and the truth. The god Pan and the Greek avenging Furies are also linked with this herb. If smoked, Juniper is said to have mild hallucino-genic properties.

Culpeper recommended Juniper as 'a counter-poison, resister of the pestilence and excellent against the biting of venomous beasts.' In herbal medicine it has been used to treat rheumatism, gout, arthritis and digestive disorders. It has antiseptic, anti-inflammatory and diuretic properties.

Juniper berries are used to add flavour to pickles, chutneys and sauces. It is the main flavouring in gin and is also brewed into a health-giving beer in Sweden. Oil of Juniper is also used in perfumes and cosmetics.

Mistletoe *(Viscum album)*

Mistletoe is a strange semi-parasitic plant that grows on various trees and derives much of the nutrients it needs by sucking these out of its host's trunk or branches. Having this unusual habit and growing between the sky and the earth made it of especial importance to the Druids and it is one of their most sacred and magical herbs. Mistletoe is found in some parts of the UK and also in Europe, Asia and North Africa. It can be easily seen in winter when the trees have lost their leaves and its evergreen clumps are made conspicuous. Mistletoe is distributed by birds that eat the berries and wipe their beaks and its sticky seeds on the branches of trees.

Its association with the Sun is because it was traditionally harvested by the Druids at Winter Solstice when it was cut down with a golden sickle with one stroke of the blade. The Mistletoe and the sickle represented the energies of the Sun and Moon, and the Druid responsible for cutting it would stand on one leg with one arm raised above him and one eye closed. This was to symbolise the between worlds association of the sacred herb, which was caught on a white cloth below to prevent it reaching the land and grounding its vital energies. It was the 'Golden Bough' of the Druids and was also mentioned in the *Aeneid* by the poet Virgil as the plant that the hero Aeneas had to remove in order to be able to enter Hades, the Underworld.

Mrs M. Grieve, in *A Modern Herbal*, informs us that:

...the curious basket of garland with which 'Jack-in-the-Green' is even now occasionally invested on May-day is said to be a relic of a similar garb assumed by the Druids for the ceremony of the Mistletoe.

She further tells us that, once they had found it, they danced around the Oak tree to the tune of Hey Derry Down, Down, Down, Derry! In Herefordshire, some Oak woods are still referred to as 'the Derry'.

Although Mistletoe grows on many trees including Apple, Hawthorn, Poplar and Ash, it was regarded as particularly magical and sacred if found on the Oak. This was the most important tree to the ancient Druids and its Celtic name 'Duir' provided the root of both 'Druid' and 'door'. The white sticky berries were thought of as the semen of the Oak tree and this caused the plant to be associated with love and fertility rituals. Its scientific name *Viscum album* echoes this because it translates as 'Sticky white'. Today the fertility association is still remembered with the traditional custom in the Yuletide season of kissing under the Mistletoe. It has also become considered a herb of 'love and peace'.

Besides being a herb of the Sun, Mistletoe is also ruled by Jupiter, and is associated with the deities Apollo, Balder, Cerridwen, Frigga, Freya, Odin and Venus. It is known as 'All Heal', 'Birdlime', 'Devil's Fuge', 'Herbe de la Croix', 'Holy Wood', 'Lignum Crucis', 'Mystyldene', 'Witch's Broom' and 'Wood of the Cross' as alternative names.

Mistletoe was once regarded as a panacea and this is why it became known as 'All Heal'. The whole plant is harvested. In herbal medicine it has been used for its diuretic and narcotic properties. Mistletoe has been employed as a remedy for high blood pressure, arthritis and epilepsy or 'falling sickness', as it used to be known. Sir John Colbatch published a pamphlet entitled *The Treatment of Epilepsy by Mistletoe* in 1720. In Sweden it was once believed that sufferers from epilepsy could prevent attacks by carrying with them a knife made with an Oak Mistletoe handle.

It has tonic properties and is useful as a treatment for spasms. Mistletoe contains histamine, choline, tyramine, viscotoxin and, as its name suggests, the last-named substance is poisonous if too much is taken. Because of its potentially toxic nature the herb should only be used under medical supervision or as prescribed by an experienced herbal medicine practitioner.

Rosemary (Rosmarinus officinalis)

Rosemary is a well-known evergreen shrub that is under the dominion of the Sun's ruling. It is highly aromatic and has its uses both for its scent as well as for its medicinal properties, and it is used in the kitchen too. Rosemary is possibly a herb of the Sun because of its liking for sunny locations. It comes from the Mediterranean coastal areas and hillsides, but is cultivated throughout the world in herb gardens.

Rosemary has small pale purplish-blue tubular flowers and its woody branches are covered in needle-like dark-green foliage. It will readily grow into quite large bushes and reach 2 metres in height.

The name Rosemary comes from the Latin *Rosmarinus*, meaning 'Dew of the Sea'. It has been a popular herb since Greek and Roman times and gained a reputation for being good for the memory and for uplifting the spirits. *Bancke's Herbal* (1525) has a long list of uses and superstitions associated with it. Anyone putting it under the bed will be 'delivered of all evill dreames'. This herbal also recommends that Rosemary should be boiled in wine as a cosmetic face-wash and that it can be bound to the legs as a treatment for gout. In Spanish folklore it is believed that Rosemary is a protection against the evil eye, and further that it once gave shelter to the Virgin Mary when its flowers took on the blue of her cloak. In Spain and Italy it is regarded as a protection from witchcraft and evil forces.

Rosemary leaves and flowering tops are the parts used, and are dried for use in cookery and in herbal medicine. The essential oil of the herb is distilled from the leaves. Rosemary can be added sparingly as a flavouring for meat and savoury dishes and in vinegar and dressings. Infusions of the herb are employed as rinses for dry hair and as a remedy for dandruff. The essential oil is used in the perfumery and cosmetic industries and the leaves can be added to pot-pourri. It was once used in place of incense and the ancients used it in religious ceremonies and rituals.

Rosemary has antiseptic and antibacterial properties and can be taken as a tea for colds, flu, fatigue and headaches. The tincture of the herb is a remedy for depression and anxiety, and as massage oil it is a treatment for rheumatism and muscular aches and pains. Rosemary is an important ingredient in the preparation of Eau-de-Cologne.

Miss Rohde praises Rosemary in *Banckes' Herbal*:

Take the Timber thereof and burn it to coals and make powder thereof and rubbe they teeth thereof and it shall keep they teeth from all evils. Smell it oft and it shall keep thee youngly.

Also if a man has lost his smelling of the ayre that he may not draw his breath, make a fire of the wood, and bake his bread therewith, eate it and it shall keep him well.

Make thee a box of the wood of Rosemary and smell to it and it shall preserve thy youth.

Rosemary is immortalised in the song Scarborough Fair by Simon and Garfunkel where they sing: 'Parsley, Sage, Rosemary and Thyme.'

St John's Wort *(Hypericum perforatum)*

St John's Wort has obvious associations with the Sun with its bright golden-yellow star-like flowers and ability to cure depression and lift the spirits. It is traditionally gathered on St John's Eve in midsummer too, when the Sun is strongest. St John's Wort is a perennial plant that comes from Europe and Asia and is naturalised in America and Australia. It grows in grassy places, hedge-banks and waste places.

St John's Wort is named after John the Baptist and it was believed that the reddish juice that exudes from its crushed flowers symbolised the saint's blood. There are many superstitions about the herb, including the belief that gathering it on St John's Eve with the dew still on it would help the picker find a husband, and if a childless wife gathered it naked, it would help her ensure conception. St John's Wort is also said to be a herb of protection that can drive away ghosts and evil spirits, as well as making sure that thunderbolts and lightning are no danger. Hanging St John's Wort in bunches at midsummer is believed to help ward off evil forces. *Hypericum* comes from the Greek and means 'over an apparition', referring to the belief that the herb was so powerful that just a whiff of the plant would make an evil spirit leave fast.

In herbal medicine St John's Wort is mainly used as an antidepressant and for combating anxiety and nervous tension. The herbalist Culpeper recommended St John's Wort as follows: 'A tincture of the flowers in spirit of wine is commended against the melancholy and madness.'

It also has antiseptic and anti-inflammatory properties and has been used externally to treat painful joints and muscular aches. The main active principle in St John's Wort is a substance known as hypericin and this is found in the flowering tops of the plant that are harvested and dried. St John's Wort is taken in the form of an infusion, but can also be made into creams, oils and other preparations. St John's Wort is often sold in capsules and tablet form in health stores where it has been marketed as the 'natural Prozac'. However, St John's Wort was banned in the Republic of Ireland some years ago. The problem is that it can interact with other medication with adverse effects, and in some people it can cause photosensitivity and skin rashes. It should not be used by pregnant women. The plant is also dangerous to livestock that may eat it when grazing.

St John's Wort has many alternative names. It is also known as 'Amber', 'Balm of Warriors', 'Bible Flower', 'Cammock', 'Goat Weed', 'Holy Herb', 'Klamath Weed', 'Penny John', 'Save', 'Sunshine Herb' and 'Tipton Weed'.

Sunflower (Helianthus annuus)
There would be something wrong if the Sunflower wasn't included in the herbs of the Sun and, of course, it is one. This spectacular annual plant can grow as high as 3 metres and bears massive flowers up to 30 centimetres across. It is so well known it hardly needs any description. It is native to North, Central and South America, but is commonly grown as a garden flower around the world and also as a crop. It is thought to have actually originated in Mexico. There are many varieties around today including the attractive cultivar Velvet Queen with brownish-orange flowers. The seeds of the Sunflower are either all-black or are white with black stripes. A single head can produce as many as 1,000 seeds in the central part of the rosette. These seeds are often used to feed captive and wild birds and the plant often springs up in all sorts of places where it has been accidentally sown.

The Sunflower's botanical name comes from the Greek 'helios' for Sun and 'anthos', which means a flower. Its flowers are just like the heavenly body the plant is named after with their golden-yellow petals like rays. If you wanted to use a herb to visualise as a symbol of the Sun, this would be ideal.

The whole plant is harvested and used to produce extracts and tinctures. The seeds and oil are a very rich source of vitamin E and are high in polyunsaturates, especially linoleic acid, which is needed by the body to maintain healthy cell membranes. It can also be used to help lower cholesterol levels. Preparations from the seeds have been used as remedies for bronchitis and coughs, and the herb has been employed externally to treat bruises and rheumatic pain. The seeds also have diuretic properties.

The Sunflower is valuable as a food source too. Its seeds can be eaten as they are or roasted and added to breads, baked products and as an ingredient in salads. Sunflower oil is used in cooking, in salad dressings and in margarine.

The Sunflower was immortalised by Vincent Van Gogh in a series of still-life paintings.

Herbs of the Moon

Nymphaeaceae Water Lily

The Moon has always been an inspiration for storytellers, poets and artists and there is surely something very magical about it. It governs the tides of the oceans of our planet and if it can exert a pull over them it is not surprising that it can have a powerful effect on us humans and many other forms of life. The Moon is associated with birth and motherhood. It is also linked with the digestive system, stomach, breasts, sympathetic nervous system and bodily fluids. The Moon is very strongly associated with the fertility of women and their monthly time of purification known as the menstrual cycle. The Moon completes its 28-day orbit around the Earth 13 times in a year, and many people are now using the 13-Moon calendar. This is a far more logical way of measuring time. This 13-Moon calendar gives us 52 weeks of seven days and a year of 364 days with the 365th being a 'day out of time'. We have lost the way of living in balance with nature and the cosmos by adopting the unnatural Gregorian calendar. It is time we all reconnected with the natural way and flows of energy of the universe. The Moon, not surprisingly, has a strong effect on our emotions and the Full Moon especially is linked with passion and madness too.

Camphor Laurel (*Cinnamomum camphora*)
Camphor is a white, waxy, very aromatic substance that mainly

14

comes from an evergreen tree that grows in Borneo, Taiwan and other parts of Asia. This very large tree is also known as the Camphor Tree and Camphorwood and it has become naturalised in many other parts of the world including Australia where it is regarded as an invasive weed.

Camphor is also found in varying amounts in several other herbs including the Camphor Basil (*Ocimum kilimandscharicum*) and Rosemary (*Rosmarinus officinalis*). The first of these plants contains as much as 61% camphor in its leaves, while Rosemary has around 20% camphor.

The word camphor is derived from the French 'camphre' that comes from the Medieval Latin 'camfora'. In ancient Sanskrit it was known as 'karpoor'.

Camphor is associated with the Moon probably because of its white and waxy appearance. It has been used in incense and this perfumed smoke rises upwards to the heavens carrying messages and prayers to the gods. Camphor is very important in Hindu religious ceremonies where it is burned. It is used in the Mahashivrati celebrations for the Lord Shiva, the god of death, destruction and renewal.

Camphor has been an important spice and aromatic resin since pre-Islamic times. It was known about and traded in Arabia at that time and is mentioned in the Koran 76:5 as flavouring for beverages. By the 13th century it was popular in many recipes and uses in the Arab world. Camphor is used today in Asian cuisine as a flavouring for desserts and in other dishes.

Camphor has its uses in herbal medicine too. It is readily absorbed through the skin and has a cooling effect when applied this way in the form of a gel. It has mild anaesthetic and antibacterial properties too. It has been combined with menthol and is a major ingredient in vapour-steam products such as Vicks VapoRub that is used as a remedy for chest infections, colds and flu. It has been used orally in small doses to treat heart problems and for fatigue. Camphor has been employed as an insect repellent as well and to help ward off other pests.

Iris (*Iris germanica var. florentina*)

The Irises are ruled by the Moon and the one most well-known and used is the Florentine Iris or Orris, as it is also known. 'Orris' is a corruption of the Greek name for the plant, which is Iris. Orris root is the powdered rhizome that has been used since the time of the ancient Egyptians because of its scent like Violets that has made it valuable in perfumery and in making pot-pourris as well as for its fixative properties. Back in the 18th century it was used in making cosmetic powders for wigs, hair and teeth. It has been associated with Florence, as its name suggests, since the 13th century when it first began to be cultivated there as an important crop. The Florentine Iris is still to be seen in the coat of arms of the Italian city.

The plant has long sword-shaped leaves that sprout from a stout rhizome and it bears white flowers tinged with mauve. It is the colour of the flowers that is probably the reason for it being in the herbs of the Moon. It comes from southern and central Europe, the Middle East and northern India.

The Florentine Iris has mild diuretic, expectorant and purgative properties, but is seldom used because it is regarded as too toxic and there are much safer and more effective remedies available. If eaten, the powered root can cause vomiting and skin rashes. The related Yellow Flag (*I. pseudocorus*) has also been occasionally used as a medicinal herb, but again is too poisonous for domestic use.

Jasmine (*Jasminum officinale*)

The word Jasmine comes from the Persian 'Yasmin', which means 'Gift from God', and with its strong perfume, delicate foliage and appearance, as well as its beautiful star-like flowers that in many species open at night, this description seems very apt. The white flowers and the way the plant's blooms come fully to life after dark are presumably why the Jasmine is regarded as a herb ruled by the Moon.

There are many species of Jasmine, which are shrubs and vines, and the genus *Jasminum* is included in the large Olive family or *Oleaceae*. Some Jasmines are evergreen and others are deciduous. The Common Jasmine (*J. officinale*), which is also known as the Poet's Jasmine and Jessamine, has been cultivated and used by people for so long that its origins are unclear, though it is thought to have come from somewhere in Central Asia. Ninth century Chinese texts say that it originated in Byzantium. Wherever the plant's original homeland was, it soon spread to many other places in the world and has been commonly grown in many parts of Europe as an ornamental garden flowering shrub. It is included in William Turner's *Names of Herbes* in 1548.

Not surprisingly, Jasmine's essential oil has been used in aromatherapy as a treatment for depression and anxiety, while because of its antiseptic and anti-inflammatory properties it has also been employed in dermatology as a remedy for sensitive skin and other complaints. Jasmine has gained a strong reputation as an aphrodisiac too.

Jasmine tea is a popular beverage in China and Japan, but is now drunk and on sale throughout the world. It is made from the flowers, but may include green tea as a base. Jasmine has been used as a flavouring in cooking. The French Jasmine syrup has found a popular use in America in scones and marshmallows. Jasmine has been very much used in perfumery and also in the making of incense.

Lettuce *(Lactuca species)*

The wild lettuces, Great Lettuce (*L. virosa*) and the Prickly Lettuce (*L. serriola*) are both used in herbal medicine and Lettuce is a herb of the Moon, although some authorities list the plants as under the dominion of Mars. All types of lettuce have white milky sap or latex and this has narcotic properties. It is probably this aspect that has given the plants an association with the Moon.

Great Lettuce can grow to around 2 metres in height and is found on roadsides, grassy banks and in waste places. It is an annual or biennial and has a branched tap root. It is native to south-western Europe and the UK, but is also found in many other parts of the world growing as a weed. It has prickly blue-green leaves and bears flower heads with small yellow blooms that look like minute Dandelions and show that the plant is in the *Compositae* or *Asteraceae* family. Prickly Lettuce is very similar, but a smaller, plant.

The white sap is known as 'Lettuce opium' and can be gathered and dried just like the more powerful drug that is obtained from the Opium Poppy (*Papaver somniferum*). It can also be used as an adulterant for this. Lettuce opium contains the alkaloid lactucarium and has similar properties to the real opium. It produces a dreamy and drowsy state if smoked and its narcotic effects have made it a herb used by recreational drug users looking for a 'legal high'. It has often been sold in 'head shops' and by suppliers of herbs that have psychoactive properties.

Mugwort *(Artemesia vulgaris)*
Mugwort is a very common perennial weed that comes from the UK, Europe, Asia and North America. It can reach over a metre in height and has grey-green jagged leaves with whitish slightly downy undersides. It bears panicles of similarly grey-green flowers with reddish-brown florets in late summer. The whole plant is aromatic if bruised. It grows in waste places, roadsides, on disturbed ground and river banks. Mugwort is a herb of the Moon and it is believed to have many magical properties. It was one of the nine herbs in the Anglo-Saxon charm against evil spirits. In Anglo-Saxon manuscripts in the Harleian collections, it is referred to as: 'The Mighty against loathed ones/That through

the land rove.' Roman soldiers believed that it would stop them having aching feet on long marches if they put the herb in their shoes. It is associated with John the Baptist and if gathered on St John's Eve the herb was thought to protect against disease and misfortune. In the Oriental macrobiotics philosophy and dietary system it is regarded as a very yang herb.

Mugwort is a close relative of Wormwood (*A. absinthium*), which is a Biblical herb known for its exceeding bitterness, and it is also a main ingredient in the mind-bending alcoholic drink absinthe, which many famous artists and writers are said to have got their inspiration from.

The leaves are harvested and dried out. They are used to make herbal tea or infusions. Mugwort is considered to be good for the digestion, as well as having stimulant properties and to be a nerve tonic. Mugwort is a remedy for diarrhoea. It is diuretic and can be used as a herb to treat menstrual problems. This would presumably be why it was regarded as ruled by the Moon. Mugwort also has insect repellent properties. It can be used as a herb that adds flavour to stuffing and sauces for meat and poultry, but it has fallen out of favour due to its potentially bitter taste. Mugwort has also been used an ingredient in brewing beer.

Water Lily *(Nymphaea alba)*

Water lilies are ruled by the Moon and the White Water Lily can be considered as representative of these plants. These lilies all have rounded leaves that float on the surface of the water like the Moon floats in the heavens above and is rounded when it is full.

Water lilies have often featured in ancient religious imagery. In the Hindu religion the gods Krishna and Brahma are often depicted with lotuses, which are another form of the plant. The Ancient Egyptians too had these lilies in much of their sacred artwork. A theory has been advanced that these people used the Egyptian Blue Water Lily (*N. caerulea*) as hallucinogens that enabled their priests and royalty to access alternative realms of the spirits and gods. On British television, Channel 4 once showed a series entitled Sacred Weeds that looked at the hallucinogenic properties of various herbs. The Blue Water Lily was examined in one episode and volunteers who had taken the plant in trials showed they were noticeably affected by the herb. They drank wine in which the flowers had been left to soak and experienced a euphoric state. Of course, we have no way of knowing how much of these plants were consumed long ago or in what way the Egyptians used them exactly, but we do know that the Egyptian Blue Water Lily has psychoactive properties.

The Tibetan Buddhist mantra of Chenrezig has been translated as: 'Hail, the jewel in the lotus.' That jewel could be the human brain's pineal gland, often thought of as the third eye, and known to be the seat of psychic visions. Deities are often shown arising from or seated in meditation in lotuses. It seems obvious this is meant to tell us something!

The Egyptian Blue Water Lily has mild sedative properties too and contains the alkaloids nuciferine and aporphine, as does the Indian Lotus or Sacred Lotus (*Nelumbo nucifera*). It has been suggested that the 'Lotus-eaters' of Homer's *Odyssey* had consumed these plants.

The White Water Lily is a perennial plant found growing in lakes, canals and slowly moving rivers in the UK and Europe. It has been used in herbal medicine for various purposes. The rootstock is the part utilised. It is astringent in its action and has been employed as a gargle to treat sore throats. It is said to have a beneficial action on the heart, liver and spleen, though has been seldom used in recent times. White Water Lily is also said to be the opposite of an aphrodisiac and its use can dampen sexual desire.

Willow (Salix alba)

The White Willow and other species of this tree have very many uses and are ruled by the Moon. They have been used in religious celebrations. In the UK, branches of willow were once used as decorations in churches and as substitute palms for Palm Sunday. In Russia there is the 'willow week', which is the week just before Easter. Willow trees have been thought of as emblems of sadness, and garlands of willow were once worn by those unlucky in love. Willow is one of the 'Nine Sacred Trees' mentioned in Wicca, and in the *Wiccan Rede* the tree is described as growing by water and a guide to the 'Summerlands' or afterlife. The willow is one of the main attributes of the Buddhist bodhisattva of compassion, the goddess Kwan Yin or Guanyin as the name is also spelled. Taoist witches are said to have used small carvings made from willow wood to aid them in communications with the dead. In China at the festival of Qingming or Tomb Sweeping, people carry willow branches with them and hang them over doorways. It is believed this practice will help drive away evil spirits at this time.

Willows root easily from cuttings and the trees are known for their tenacity to life. There is a story that says that the poet Alexander Pope once begged a twig of willow from a parcel that had been tied up with such twigs and sent from Spain to Lady Suffolk. The twig was planted and grew so well that the legend goes that all British Weeping Willows (*S. x sepulcralis*) are descended from it.

Willow wood is very pliant and strong at the same time. It has been used to make all sorts of objects, tools and furniture items ranging from cricket bats, brooms and chairs to whistles, flutes and poles, as well as wands for magical use. Willow shoots and split Willow rods can be used in basket-making.

Willow is the source of salicylic compounds. Acetylsalicylic acid is more commonly known and marketed as aspirin, and is used for its analgesic, anti-rheumatic and fever-reducing properties. Willow bark can also be used to provide relief from pain and to treat colds and flu, and this was the traditional way of using the tree as a medicinal herb. Today most aspirin has been chemically synthesised. It is an excellent example of how many modern drugs have their origins in wild plants and herbal treatments.

Herbs of Mercury

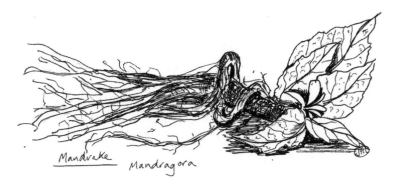

Mandrake   Mandragora

Mercury is associated with speed and agility. Quicksilver is another name for the element. Mercury is thought of as the messenger for the other gods. The keyword of Mercury is communication.

Dill *(Anethum graveolens)*

Dill is a herb ruled by Mercury that is very similar to its cousin Fennel (described below), but a much smaller plant. Like its relative, it is used both for culinary and medicinal purposes. It grows to about 1 metre in height and has feathery aromatic foliage and umbels of small yellowish flowers. Dill is grown in herb gardens worldwide, but is thought to have originated in southern Europe and Asia.

The seeds and leaves are the parts that are used. Poultices are made from the foliage and used to treat boils, swellings and joint pains. The seeds are chewed as a remedy for bad breath and as a main ingredient in 'gripe water' that is given to babies for indigestion. Dill has soothing and cooling properties and is good for the digestive system and preventing constipation.

In cooking, the seeds are added to curries, soups, rice dishes, pickles and chutneys. Dill is also good with fish, seafood and egg dishes, and to add flavour to mild-tasting vegetables such as potatoes and cucumber.

Dill was used in Biblical times and by the Greeks and Romans. In Anglo-Saxon times it was believed to be of use against witchcraft, and if burned it was thought to be able to 'disperse thunder clouds and sulphurous air'.

Culpeper informs us that:

Mercury has the dominion of this plant, and therefore to be sure it strengthens the brain... It stays the hiccough, being boiled in wine, and but smelled into being tied in a cloth. The seed is of more use than the leaves, and more effectual to digest raw and vicious humours, and is used in medicines that serve to expel wind, and the pains proceeding therefrom...

Fennel *(Foeniculum vulgare)*

The popular medicinal and culinary herb Fennel is a herb of Mercury. Perhaps this is not surprising because this pretty plant cannot fail to communicate. Its delicate ferny leaves are a joy to look at and crushed they give off a delightful aroma like Aniseseed. Fennel is in the *Apiaceae* or Parsley family and bears umbels of yellowish flowers on tall stalks that rise above the foliage. It grows in many parts of the world and can be found on rough ground as well as on roadsides and by the sea.

In herbal medicine it is used as a diuretic and an expectorant. It is also believed to be an aid to slimming as well as being a tonic for the eyesight. It is usually taken as a herb tea or an infusion made from the seeds. Such a brew can be used to bathe the eyes as a treatment for conjunctivitis.

The finely-cut leaves can be used to add flavour to sauces and are ideal with oily fish dishes. The seeds are ideal as flavouring for curries and spicy sauces.

There is an old rhyme which states that: 'Fennel, Vervain, Mugwort and Dill hinder witches of their will.' This doesn't make that much sense though when you consider that practitioners of witchcraft often use all these herbs. Fennel is also said to be a good herb of protection that will help ward off evil spirits.

Lavender *(Lavandula angustifolia)*
Lavender is another herb ruled by Mercury that is a plant that definitely communicates with its perfume, pretty flowers and very many uses. Lavender has stimulating properties too, which would fit with the quickness of Mercury.

Lavender is an aromatic and hardy shrub from the Mint and Sage family, or the *Lamiaceae* or *Labiatae*, as this large group of plants is known to botanists. It has tiny purple-blue flowers carried in spikes above the bush of foliage below. There are many species of Lavender as well as hybrids and cultivars, but most have purplish flowers, although not all types are aromatic. There are also some white and pink-flowered cultivars. Lavender likes a lot of sunlight and the plant originated in the Mediterranean and Middle East. There are endemic species found in the Canary Islands too.

The highly perfumed Lavenders are used in commercial perfumery and in making pot-pourris. The flowers are dried and put in little sachets or bags that can be stored among clothing to help deter moths and to scent the garments. Lavender essential oil can be added to the bathwater or included as an ingredient in homemade cosmetics.

Lavender has medicinal uses too. Weak infusions of the flowers can be used to treat anxiety and nervous exhaustion. The essential oil diluted in carrier oil can be applied to sunburn, burns, scalds, and as massage oil for relieving migraine, tension headaches and muscular aches and pains. Inhaling the fragrance of Lavender flowers can be a good way to treat insomnia and anxiety because the aroma is very calming. The herb has been found to have antibacterial and antiseptic properties and is also used in aromatherapy.

Lavender has its uses too in the kitchen. The flowers can add flavour to sugar used in making cakes, biscuits, meringues, ice-cream and desserts. Flowers can also be added to jam, vinegar or cooked (tied in a muslin bag) with blackcurrants and other soft fruit.

Lavender is such a well-known and traditionally used herb that it is in the Lavender's Blue nursery rhyme.

Lemon Verbena (Aloysia citriodora)

Lemon Verbena is a half-hardy shrub that is very popular because of its lemon-scented foliage. In Victorian times it was known as the 'Lemon Plant' and its leaves were dried and put into sachets for their perfume. Its botanical name *Aloysia* is believed to be a corruption of Louisa, and that it was named after Maria Louisa, the wife of King Carlos IV of Spain. In Spanish today the herb is known as 'Hierba Luisa'.

Lemon Verbena came originally from Chile and Argentina, but is grown nowadays in many subtropical parts of the world. It forms a large bush and can reach as much as 4 metres in height in ideal conditions, but is usually seen a lot smaller than this. It bears flowering spikes of tiny mauve-white flowers in summer.

Lemon Verbena leaves, fresh or dried, can be used to make a herbal tea and also to add flavour to cakes and ice-cream or in savoury stuffings and sauces. The scent and lemon flavour are very strong though, so they should be used with discretion.

Lemon Verbena, like the other herbs of Mercury we have looked at so far, has a strong perfume that stimulates the senses. This property has made it very popular as an ingredient in pot-pourri.

Mandrake (Mandragora officinarum)

The Mandrake is a very strange herb that has not surprisingly been the subject of many superstitious beliefs. One of which is that the plant can scream when it is pulled up and that its unearthly cry could drive anyone hearing it insane or even kill them. In *Romeo and Juliet*, Shakespeare wrote: 'And shrieks like mandrake's torn out of the earth that living mortals hearing them run mad.' In *Henry VI*, Part 2, he wrote: 'Would curses kill as doth the mandrakes groan.'

The herbalist Gerard, however, did not believe in the superstitions surrounding the Mandrake and wrote:

> There have been many ridiculous tales brought up of this plant, whether of old wives or runnegate surgeons or phisick mongers, I know not, al which dreames and old wives tales you shall from henceforth cast out your bookes of memorie.

A safe way of digging up a Mandrake was to tie the plant to a hungry dog and then tempt the animal to make for a dish of meat. As it did so it pulled the root out of the ground and would die instead of the human who had gone out of reach of the danger. Once the Mandrake was out of the ground it was believed to be safe to handle.

It is probably this superstition that caused the Mandrake to be included in the herbs ruled by Mercury because if it could scream out it could clearly communicate! If it is consumed, the plant has hallucinogenic properties too because it contains the toxic tropane alkaloids atropine and hyoscyamine, which are also found in its relatives the Deadly Nightshade (*Atropa belladonna*) and Henbane (*Hyoscyamus niger*) respectively. These herbs from the *Solanaceae* are very poisonous and while they have been used in witchcraft, the danger is too great to risk taking them. Mandrake used to be used as a powerful sedative and as an anaesthetic painkiller. In Greek and Roman times it was used to knock a patient out who was undergoing surgery.

Mandrake's very long forked roots look a bit like legs and so the herb was thought to resemble small men and was often depicted this way in illustrations. Pythagoras is said to have referred to the Mandrake as an 'anthropomorph', which means a tiny man. In France the herb became associated with the elf

Mandelgloire, a supernatural being that was believed to have the power of being able to bring wealth. In the trial of Joan of Arc, she was accused of having a Mandrake in the form of a manikin that she used for witchcraft. The dried roots were once used as magical amulets that were thought to protect the wearer from evil. This led to a trade in the roots and also fake Mandrake charms, which were often fashioned out of Bryony roots as well.

Turner alluded to this practice when he wrote: 'They are so trimmed of crafty theves to mocke the poore people withal and to rob them both of theyr wit and theyr money.'

However, he said of the Mandrake:

Of the apples of the Mandrake, if a man smell of them thei will make hym slepe and also if they be eaten. But they that smell to much of the apples become dum...thys herbe diverse wayes taken is very jepardus for a man and may kill hym if he eat it or drynk it out of measure and have no remedy from it... If mandragora be taken out of measure, by and by slepe ensueth and a great lousing of the streyngthe with a forgetfulness.

The Mandrake has been thought to have aphrodisiac powers too and to be able to increase fertility and attract lovers if it is worn as an amulet. In the *Book of Genesis*, Rachel barters with Leah for her son's Mandrake roots because she wanted to use them to be able to conceive her own child.

It used to be believed, too, that there were Mandrakes of both sexes. The 'Womandrake' has been identified as the related *M. autumnalis* species, which has purplish flowers. William Turner, the Dean of Wells (c.1508-68) claimed in his 16th century herbal that the female plant's fruit was 'well smelling', whereas that of the male Mandrake 'did smell pleasantly joined to a certain grevousness'.

The Mandrake is a perennial low-growing herb that forms a rosette of ovate leaves around its rootstock. It is said to have originated in the Himalayas and parts of the Mediterranean, but became introduced to many other countries. It grows best in full sunlight and in sandy soil. The Mandrake has clusters of greenish-white flowers that are followed by large green fruits that turn yellow as they ripen. These fruits are known as 'Devil's Apples', an apt name considering their poisonous nature.

Mint (Mentha)

Mint is another herb that Mercury rules over. The strong minty smell certainly communicates to us so perhaps that is why it was chosen to have this planetary ruler. Or perhaps, in keeping with the speed of Mercury, because many types of Mint can spread rapidly by sending out runners. There are some 25 species of Mint as well as many hybrids, and all are useful herbs that are widely cultivated.

The Romans put Mint in their bathwater and used it in perfumes and the classical poet Ovid recommended that boards used for food preparation should be scoured with 'green mint' before being set out as offerings to the gods. Mercury was the messenger for his fellow deities so again there is a connection here.

It was the Romans too who introduced the Spearmint (*M. spicata*) to Britain where by the 16th century it had become a popular strewing herb, as well as being used for other purposes. This is the species that goes into mint sauce and mint jelly, as well as being added to salads and many savoury dishes. Mint can be a flavouring for yogurt as well as a garnish for drinks and an ingredient for herb teas. The Peppermint (*M. x piperita*) is popular as a natural flavour in sweets, chocolate, desserts, ice-cream, cordials, in icing and cake. Away from the kitchen, Peppermint gets used in chewing gum and in toothpastes. Spearmint is good for the digestion and Peppermint is a treatment for colds. The essential oil is a decongestant, as well as being antiseptic. As an inhalant it can be used as a remedy for chest infections, catarrh and asthma. Mints are popular ingredients in pot-pourri, as well as in many household products.

Other popular mints include Gingermint (*M. x gracilis* 'Variegata'), Pineapple Mint (*M. suaveolens* 'Variagata'), and Eau-de-Cologne Mint (*M. x piperita citrata*). This last variety comes as Orange, Lemon or Bergamot Mint and has a definite citrus scent while also being reminiscent of Lavender water.

The Mints are hardy perennial herbs that do best in moist conditions and they are propagated by division and root cuttings. They are found worldwide nowadays and are cultivated both as garden plants and as crops.

Valerian (*Valeriana officinalis*)

Valerian has no obvious links with Mercury, however, this herb has tranquillising and sedative properties that can help send someone who suffers from insomnia into the world of dreams, and what are dreams, but messages from the subconscious. Valerian brings the body into a state of relaxation and so helps communication with the dream-world.

Valerian grows to a metre or more in height and bears clusters of pale pink flowers from June to August. It has finely cut pinnate leaves and underground it has a short rhizome with fibrous rootlets. This is the part of the plant that is harvested in autumn and dried. Valerian comes from Europe and Asia, but is now grown in many other parts of the world. In its natural habitat it is found in ditches, by rivers and streams and in damp grassy places.

Besides being used as a remedy for insomnia and nervous conditions it has been used to treat headaches and to relieve spasms. The root has a very strong smell, which many people find unpleasant and hence its alternative name of Fu or Phew. It has nevertheless been used in perfumery.

The name *Valeriana* is derived from the Latin verb *valere*, meaning to be in good health, and the herb was once regarded as a panacea. In Medieval times it was called All-Heal. Today it is often sold in health stores and from herbal supplement suppliers as a remedy for anxiety and insomnia. Some people, however, claim that it can be just as addictive as pharmaceutical sedatives and tranquillisers.

Culpeper praised Valerian as an herbal medicine and wrote:

> The root boiled with liquorice, raisons and aniseed is good for those troubled with cough. Also, it is of special value against the plague, the decoction thereof being drunk and the root smelled. The green herb being applied to the head taketh away pain and pricking thereof.

Valerian contains chatinine and actinidine and these substances are both 'cat psychoactive', which means that the animals are attracted and enchanted by the plant just as happens with Catnip. The smell of the roots of Valerian has a euphoric effect on them and they will roll around happily when under its spell. Rats are affected by the smell of the herb too and it has been suggested that the Pied Piper of Hamelin held his mysterious power over the animals because he was carrying Valerian roots.

Valerian has been used as an ingredient in love potions and also in Voodoo magic. It is known to Voodoo practitioners as 'Graveyard Dust', and another name for the plant is 'Herb of Witches'.

Herbs of Venus

Rose
rosaceae

Venus is the goddess of love and her keyword is harmony. Anything to do with feelings and sensuality could be described as Venusian, and beauty and a feminine influence would also come as part of a list of characteristics of anything ruled over by the planet Venus.

Catnip/Catmint (*Nepeta cataria*)

Catnip or Catmint is a perennial herb from the Labiatae family that is often grown in gardens because of its attractive mauve-purple flowers and its grey-green foliage. It is frequently culti-vated too because it has a strange power of attraction over cats and hence its descriptive names. This is presumably why it is a herb ruled over by Venus. Our feline friends love it. They will roll about ecstatically in clumps of the plant and the dried herb is often put as a stuffing material in toys that are sold for cats because of its powers of keeping the animals happy.

Catnip is also said to have an effect on humans if it is smoked when it can produce a mild-marijuana-like high. It can be taken as a herbal tea too and it has a tranquillising and mildly sedative action. Catnip also lowers fevers and increases perspiration. The herb has been used as a remedy for colds, influenza, flatulence and digestive disorders, anaemia, amenorrhoea and other women's complaints.

Although it has a calming effect on people if smoked or taken as tea, an old saying advises that, 'if the root be chewed it will make the most quiet person fierce and quarrelsome'.

Catnip originates in Europe, Asia and Africa, but has been introduced to North America and many other temperate zones. It can be found growing wild in grassy places with chalky soils, on roadsides and at the edges of fields.

Columbine *(Aquilegia vulgaris)*
The Columbine is a pretty garden flower from the *Ranunculaceae* or Buttercup family that comes in many colours such as purple, pink and white, and is well known to gardeners throughout the world. It is a herb ruled by Venus because its English name is derived from 'columba', which is the Latin for dove, a bird that is associated with peace, love and harmony. At the same time its scientific name *Aquilegia* comes from the Latin for eagle, which is 'aquila'. So the Columbine combines the fierceness of the eagle with the gentleness of the dove!

There are actually many related species of Columbine and the plants are found in the wild in meadows and woods throughout the Northern Hemisphere. The Colorado Blue Columbine (*A. caerulea*) is the state flower of Colorado. Columbines are perennial plants that grow to about 60 centimetres in height and they will readily self-seed if grown in gardens.

Small quantities of the roots of Columbine have been used by some American Indians as a remedy for ulcers, and the plant has been also been employed as a treatment for jaundice and diseases of the liver. However, it is generally considered to be too toxic and is no longer used in herbal medicine apart from in homeopathy where it is sometimes prescribed for hysteria and nervous disorders.

Culpeper wrote:

The leaves of Columbine are successfully used in lotions for sore mouths and throats... The Spaniards used to eat a piece of the root thereof in a morning fasting many days together, to help them when troubled with stone. The seed taken in wine with a little saffron removes obstructions of the liver and is good for the yellow jaundice.

Pennyroyal *(Mentha pulegium)*

Pennyroyal is a medicinal herb from the Mint family that grows in the wild in damp places and along streams. One of its alternative names is Lurk-in-the-Ditch. It is a perennial plant that creeps along the ground and bears its whorls of lilac flowers on stalks carried above the foliage. The whole plant is aromatic and has a minty, but antiseptic smell. There is an upright variety of the plant as well known as the *'erecta'* form, while the creeping version is known as *'procumbens'*. Pennyroyal is found in North America, Canada and parts of Europe, but should not be confused with American or Mock Pennyroyal (*Hedeoma pulegoides*).

Pennyroyal contains menthol and pulegone as essential oils and is used in herbal medicine as a sedative, for relieving spasms, and to counter migraine and digestive disorders. It is brewed into an infusion or tea, but is said to be able to cause miscarriage so should never be used by pregnant women.

The late Kurt Cobain of the rock band Nirvana wrote a song entitled Pennyroyal Tea, which was included on the album In Utero in 1993. In *Cobain's Journals*, published posthumously in 2002, the star gave this explanation for what his song was about: 'herbal abortive... it doesn't work, you hippie.' However, in a previous interview in the October 1993 issue of *Impact* he claimed it was about a severely depressed person.

In the times of the Ancient Greeks, Pennyroyal was an ingredient in 'Kykeon', a drink that was consumed at the climax of the

Eleusinian Mysteries that resulted in mystical experiences. It was also added to wine by the Greeks and both these people and the Romans used Pennyroyal as a culinary herb. It was still used in cooking as late as the Middle Ages, but has fallen out of favour due to its potentially toxic properties. Speaking of Pennyroyal's poisonous nature, it has often been used as an insecticide and repellent against fleas and other pests.

Pennyroyal is believed to be a herb of immortality and according to a folklore tradition it can be used to calm stormy seas. Perhaps these are some of the reasons it is regarded as a herb of Venus?

Periwinkle *(Vinca major/minor)*

The Periwinkles, both Greater and Lesser ('major and 'minor') are perennial evergreen herbs that grow in woods and shaded areas in the wild, but are widely cultivated as ornamental garden plants in many parts of the world. They are used as trailing ground-cover and look very attractive with their blue flowers and contrasting dark green leaves. An alternative name for the Periwinkle is 'Blue Buttons'. They have also been called the Sorcerer's Violet, hinting at their magical properties.

The Lesser Periwinkle comes from Central Europe and Western Asia, while the Greater Periwinkle is from the Mediterranean, but the plants have been naturalised in many other places.

Periwinkle contains the alkaloid vincamine and has been used in herbal medicine to treat vertigo, tinnitus, headache, hearing problems and disorders of the brain. However, due to its potentially toxic nature it is not for domestic use. In homeopathy it is prescribed as a remedy for bleeding and skin rashes. In 1923, much interest was aroused in the Periwinkle as a potential treatment for diabetes, and that it could possibly be used as a substitute for insulin.

Culpeper recommended Periwinkle in this way, stating that

Periwinkle:

> ...stays bleeding at the mouth and nose, if it be chewed...and may be used with advantage in hysteric and other fits... It is good in nervous disorders, the young tops made into a conserve is good for the night-mare. The small periwinkle possesses all the virtues of the other kind, and may very properly supply its place.

Periwinkle is a herb of Venus because of its many associations with love and passion, as well as its magical properties. It has been an ingredient in love potions and spells. The 14th century *Boke of Secrets of Albertus Magnus* tells of a recipe in which it is wrapped with earthworms, mixed with Houseleeks (*Sempervivum*), reduced to a powder and then eaten with a meal to make a man and wife love each other more. It is said that if Periwinkle is sprinkled under a couple's bed, it will increase the desire for love-making between them, and that if they both eat the flower of this herb it will have an aphrodisiac effect. This is probably not a good idea though because the Periwinkle is a poisonous plant. This is possibly why it is also linked with death and funerals, for which it is used in wreaths, and earning it the name 'Flower of Death'. Periwinkle was mentioned by Pliny as a herb that was woven into garlands in ancient Greece and Rome.

The ancient herbalist Apuleius, in his *Herbarium* (printed 1480) gave complex details for the gathering of the herb:

> This wort is of good advantage for many purposes, that is to say, first against devil sickness and demoniacal possessions and against snakes and wild beasts and against poisons and for various wishes and for envy and terror and that thou mayst have grace, and if thou have the wort with thee thou shalt be prosperous and ever acceptable. This wort thou shalt pluck thus, saying, 'I pray thee, vinca pervinca, thee that art to

be had for they many useful qualities, that thou come to me glad blossoming with thy mainfulness, that thou outfit me so that I be shielded and ever prosperous and undamaged by poisons and by water'; when thou shalt pluck this wort, thou shalt be clean of every uncleaness, and thou shalt pick it when the moon is nine nights old and eleven nights and thirteen nights and thirty nights and when it is one night old.

Periwinkle is also a herb of the Mother Goddess and has its place in women's magical rituals. It is also seen as a herb of protection that can ward off evil if it is hung over a doorway. *Macer's Herbal*, published in the 11th century, claimed that Periwinkle had power against 'wykked spirits'.

Periwinkle found its place in the writings of the poets too. Wordsworth wrote: 'Though primrose tufts in that sweet bower, The fair periwinkle trailed its wreaths.'

Rose (Rosa)

It is probably no surprise to you to learn that the Rose is included in the herbs governed by the goddess and the planet Venus. The Rose has become a symbol for matters of the heart. This beautiful flower has been associated with love and romance for a very long time and the ancient Greeks and Romans identified it with their goddesses of love, Aphrodite and Venus. The Rose has often been used as an ingredient in love potions and spells to attract a lover.

There are many species of Rose and hybrids and varieties that are popular in gardening. Everyone knows what a Rose looks like so there is really no need for a physical description.

The Rose has many legends about it and magical attributes that add to its status as a herb of love and a mystical flower. Early Christians believed that the five petals of the Rose represented the five wounds of Christ. Red Roses became associated with the blood of martyrs and the flower also became identified with the Virgin Mary. The Rose is an important symbol in heraldry too. It is the national flower of England. A red Rose held in the hand is a symbol for socialism. A bouquet of the flowers in this colour is used to show true love and is a traditional gift on Valentine's Day. The Rose Cross is the symbol for the mystical Rosicrucian order.

There is the legend that the original Rose that grew in the Biblical Garden of Eden was white, but it turned red as it blushed due to the shame of Adam and Eve's sin and fall from grace.

Roses have their uses in herbal medicine too. Rose hips are often made into jam, jelly and syrup and are an excellent source of vitamin C. Rose essential oil is used in aromatherapy for depression and anxiety. Rose petals and hips are recommended as a treatment for colds, bronchitis and gastric problems. It is important that the rough seeds in the hips are not swallowed though because they can cause irritation and have been ground up to make 'itching powder'.

Distilled rose-water is used to flavour confectionery such as Turkish delight. Dried petals and flower-buds can be added to pot-pourri and the essential oil of Rose adds its perfume to many beauty products.

Culpeper had a lot to say in praise of the Rose and tells us:

Of the Red Roses are usually made many compositions, all serving to sundry good uses, viz. electuary of roses, conserve both moist and dry, which is usually called sugar of roses, syrup of dry roses and honey of roses; the cordial powder called aromatic rosarum, the distilled water of roses, vinegar of roses, ointment and oil of roses and the rose leaves dried are of very great use and effect.

The last word about the Rose can go to Shakespeare who wrote:

With sweet musk roses and with eglantine
There sleeps Titania, sometime of the night
Lull'd in these flowers with dances and delight.

Vervain *(Verbena officinalis)*

Vervain is a perennial herb with spindly stalks and dainty lilac-coloured flowers carried in spikes. It often grows as a weed and in waste places, roadsides, railway banks and along paths and can reach 1 metre in height though is often smaller. It comes from much of Europe, Asia and North Africa, but has been introduced elsewhere and is grown in herb gardens around the world.

It is very much a herb of Venus because the Romans believed it was sacred to this goddess, and also used it as an 'altar plant'. Since then it has been a popular herb for love spells and potions and is regarded as a traditional aphrodisiac.

In the Bible it was used by King Solomon for purifying his temple, and it was regarded as a holy plant by the Hebrews, Egyptians and Greeks. The Druids regarded Vervain as one of the most important magical herbs and it was an ingredient in their 'lustral water'. It was used in ritual cleansings and as a herb of protection and good luck. It was an aid to divination, especially when gathered at the time of rising of Sirius the Dog Star, when there was no light from Sun or Moon. Initiation is described in the Chair of Taliesin bardic poem, and a drink is made in which Vervain is an important magical ingredient. It is also an important herb in the Cauldron of Cerridwen, the cauldron of the Celtic shape-shifter goddess. Besides Venus, Vervain is also associated with Aphrodite, Diana, Horus, Isis, Ra, Thor and Zeus.

Vervain is regarded as an aid to inspiration for poets, singers and mystics, and can be taken to enhance clairvoyant ability. It is said that the Pawnee Indians used Vervain for similar purposes, believing that it improved dreaming.

Vervain was reputed to have grown on Mount Calvary where it was gathered and used to staunch the blood of Christ's wounds. This gave the plant the name 'Herb of the Cross'. It is also known as 'Enchanter's Plant', 'Herb of Enchantment', 'Herb of Grace', 'Holy Herb', 'Simpler's Joy' and 'Wizard's Plant'.

Vervain is used in herbal medicine as a tranquilliser to treat nervous conditions and insomnia. The flowering stems are dried and the herb is utilised to make infusions. It has astringent and diuretic properties too and has also been employed as a remedy for rheumatism, migraine, headaches, digestive disorders, kidney, liver and gallbladder problems and skin diseases. The leaves can be used to make a hair tonic and eyewash. In homeopathy it is prescribed for cases of epilepsy.

Despite its rather weak and unspectacular appearance, Vervain is truly a herb with very many uses and it has found itself as the focus of a wealth of superstitions and beliefs.

Yarrow (Achillea millefolium)

Yarrow or Milfoil is a perennial herb found growing in grassy places in Europe, Asia and naturalised in North America, Australia and New Zealand. It has finely divided leaves and its name *millefolium* means 'thousand leaves'. The *Achillea* part of its name is from Achilles the legendary hero whose soldiers were said to have staunched their bleeding wounds with this herb while fighting in the Trojan War.

Yarrow is a herb ruled by Venus with some very obvious reasons. It is associated with true love and features in a number of spells and magical rhymes. One folk saying goes: 'Yarrow, yarrow, long and narrow, Tell unto me by tomorrow, Who my husband is to be.'

Another version of this, in which an ounce of Yarrow is sewed up in flannel and placed underneath the pillow before going to bed, after repeating the following words, goes: 'Thou pretty herb of Venus' tree, Thy true name it is Yarrow; Now who my bosom friend must be, Pray tell thou me to-morrow.' (Halliwel's *Popular Rhymes*)

Another rhyme, said to come from Suffolk, also refers to its ability to cause a nosebleed, in this case as sign of love: 'Green 'arrow, green 'arrow, you bears a white blow, If my love loves me my nose will bleed now.'

There is a superstition that claimed that if Yarrow was eaten at a wedding feast then the bride and groom would remain faithful for seven years.

One of the other keywords of Venus is harmony and balance, and Yarrow has traditionally been used when consulting the I-Ching Oriental system of divination. A bundle of 50 stalks of Yarrow are employed to consult the Book of Changes as the I-Ching is also known.

Yarrow bears creamy-white to pinkish flower heads that are carried on flowering stalks about 30 centimetres in height or more. It has creeping roots and can be an invasive weed in lawns and fields.

Yarrow is an aromatic herb with a number of medicinal uses. It is applied externally to treat wounds, ulcers and nosebleeds, which it is said to heal as well as cause. Yarrow has anti-inflammatory properties and it increases perspiration. Taken as a herbal tea it is a remedy for colds and fevers, and is also recommended for indigestion and lowering blood pressure. The flowering tops made into an infusion in distilled water can be used as a skin cleanser and conditioner for oily complexions.

Yarrow leaves can also be used sparingly in soups and salads to add their peppery and spicy flavour.

Yarrow has many other superstitions centred on it. The herb was once known as 'Devil's Plaything' and 'Devil's Nettle' because it was supposedly dedicated to Satan. It was often used in spells and charms and found its place in Druid ceremonies too. It could be fashioned into herbal amulets and strewn on the threshold of a house as it was believed it would offer protection against evil. A bunch of Yarrow hung over a doorway or attached to a baby's crib on Midsummer's Eve was thought to bring an illness-free year ahead. In the 15th century *Book of Secrets* by Albertus Magnus it was revealed that Yarrow applied to the nose would protect 'from all feare and fatansye or vision'.

Herbs of Mars

Dragon Tree
dracaena draco

Mars is the god of war and rules the zodiac sign of Aries. This means that to be pioneering, energetic and a leader are all characteristics that are key to this planetary ruler, as well as aggression, and the use of weapons and sharp tools. The masculine influence is a big part of Mars too. Mars is also linked with passion, with heat, with the colour red and with blood. Any herbs ruled by Mars should show some of these qualities and characteristics.

Dragon Tree (*Dracaena draco*)

The Dragon Tree, which comes from Tenerife, Gran Canaria and La Palma in the Canary Islands as well as Cape Verde, Madeira and Morocco, has many obvious signs as to why it was regarded as a herb of Mars. This curious plant that grows into a definite tree as it matures has long leathery and spiky leaves that form in rosettes at the top of its trunk and branches. Their sharp points make this an aggressive-looking tree. If it is cut it bleeds a resinous sap that becomes a dark red as it is exposed to the air. This is the 'dragon's blood' that has been used in incense and in the occult for anything to do with Mars. The Dragon Tree is also a pioneering plant that will grow in hot arid landscapes and even on rocky cliffs. Its berries are an orange-red too.

The most famous Dragon Tree in the world is the 'Drago Milenario', which is said to be between 1,000 and 3,000 years old. It is a focal point in the city of Icod de los Vinos in Tenerife and stands in its own Parque de Drago ('Park of the Dragon Tree'). Countless tourists pay a visit to this ancient tree, which has become a plant symbol for the island.

It is said that the Guanche people, who were the original residents of the Canary Islands before the Spanish Conquest, used to hold important meetings under this particular Dragon Tree, and looking at the size of it this is easy to believe. It is also said that the Guanches made shields out of the bark and trunk of Dragon Trees. Its use as a weapon, if only of defence, would be another reason why it is a herb of Mars.

The Dragon Tree has been used as a medicinal herb since Roman times because its red sap, once dried and ground into powder, is thought to be good for bleeding gums and sores in the mouth, as well as strengthening the teeth. It is also used as a treatment for ulcers and haemorrhages. The dragon's blood has been used to impart its colour into varnishes and dyes too as well as in the production of lacquers.

Dragon Trees are often grown in gardens and parks today, but are very rare in the wild and the plant is a protected species. Some of the very large and ancient trees take on strange forms with their massive trunks and mushroom or fan-shaped heads of smaller branches, each crowned with a rosette of spiky leaves. The tree will also put down aerial roots and has been likened to the dragon Ladon of legend that was said to guard the Gardens of the Hesperides. This fabulous beast had 100 heads and this is why the Dragon Tree's form with so many branches on top of the main trunk has been likened to it. The aerial roots have also been likened to a dragon's beard. In the myth Ladon was killed by

Atlas and where the mighty reptile's blood fell Dragon Trees sprung up.

Galangal (Alpinia officinarum)

Lesser Galangal is a relative of the Ginger and like this spice it has a hot flavour, though a lot milder than its cousin. It is used in Thai and Asian cooking. Galangal has reddish ginger-scented rhizomes and the colouring of its roots as well as its spicy flavour are the characteristics that have made it a herb ruled by Mars. Its name comes from the Arabic word 'khalanjan' that is thought to be a corruption of the Chinese for 'mild ginger'. The plant is also known as 'Blue Ginger'. The Arabs, by the way, are said to have used Galangal to make their horses fiery in spirit, so this would be another reason why it comes under the dominion of Mars.

Galangal comes from the tropical rainforest of Southeast Asia and produces clumps of lance-shaped leaves that can reach over a metre in height. It has white flowers that may have green or purplish tinges. There is also the larger species A. galanga, which is the Greater Galangal and reaches as much as 2 metres in height, though has a much milder flavour.

Besides its use in cooking, Galangal has medicinal properties too. It is antibacterial and antifungal, as well as being good for the digestion. Galangal mixed with lime juice is regarded as a tonic in some parts of Southeast Asia. It has been recommended as a remedy for seasickness and to prevent vomiting. Galangal in powdered form has been used as snuff in India. It is a popular spice and medicine in Lithuania and Estonia, and was made into a herb tea in Russia.

Galangal root is a stimulant and mild hallucinogen. The rhizome is chewed or the roots are brewed as an infusion. One tablespoonful of the rhizome is used with half a pint of boiling water. It has also been used as an ingredient in incense to increase physical and magical energy.

Hops *(Humulus lupulus)*

Hops are best known as a vital ingredient in brewing beer and that is why this climbing perennial hardy herb is grown as a crop. It also has its uses in herbal medicine as well. Hops are found in many parts of Europe, Asia and North America and grow in hedges, thickets and waste places where they can find something to twine their hairy climbing stems around.

The Hop plant is ruled by Mars and this is probably due to its aggressive nature; Hops can strangle other species they twine around as they grow. Pliny made reference to this when he called the plant 'Lupus salictarius', which translates as 'Willow wolf' and describes how Hops can kill this tree. 'Lupus' means wolf in Latin and *'lupulus'* is in the plant's scientific name.

Herbalist John Evelyn, in *Pomona* (1670), wrote a word of warning when he said:

Hops transmuted our wholesome ale into beer, which doubtless much alters its constitution. This one ingredient, by some suspected not unworthily, preserves the drink indeed, but repays the pleasure in tormenting diseases and a shorter life.

Hops grow as both male and female plants. The male flowers are in inconspicuous clusters, whereas the female flowers are pale green cone-like inflorescences and are the part harvested as Hops that are dried and used in the brewing industry.

Hops are in the Hemp family or *Cannabinaceae* and it is possible to graft a Hop onto a Cannabis rootstock. Such a plant looks like a Hop, but contains varying amounts of THC – the illegal drug found in Marijuana.

Hops contain humulene and lupulin and have a tranquillising or sedative effect. Because of this, dried Hops can be stuffed into herb pillows to bring relief to those people who suffer from insomnia. Hops also have antibacterial properties. Made into an infusion, Hops can be taken as a remedy for anxiety and nervous problems, and externally is a treatment for skin conditions.

Young shoots of the Hop plant can be cooked as greens and eaten like Asparagus shoots.

Meadow Buttercup *(Ranunculus acris)*

The common Meadow Buttercup is a herb of Mars despite its pretty golden-yellow flowers. The reason is given in the *'acris'* part of its name because this means 'acrid' and so it is. The juice of the plant contains the toxin Ranunculin and causes inflammation and blistering. Even pulling it up and carrying the bruised stems in a bare hand can cause soreness and blisters to form. Grazing cattle will do their best to avoid eating Buttercups growing in fields and pastures they are feeding from.

Meadow Buttercups have, however, been used in herbal medicine as a cure for warts. The juice from the leaves is so caustic that it can burn the growths away.

The Meadow Buttercup comes from Europe and Asia, but is now naturalised in many temperate parts of the world where it is regarded as a weed.

Tarragon *(Artemesia dracunculus)*

Tarragon is a herb of Mars, possibly because of its association with dragons. Its scientific name *dracunculus* means 'little dragon' in Latin. The plant was once believed to have had the magical power of being able to cure the bite of a venomous serpent or a mad dog.

Tarragon is a perennial that reaches around 1 metre in height and is covered in aromatic pointed leaves that grow from its branching stems. It produces clusters of insignificant grey-green flowers, but only in very warm conditions. It comes from Southern Europe originally, but is grown in herb gardens in many parts of the world. It is a close relative of the Wormwood (*A. absinthium*), which is also ruled by Mars.

John Evelyn in his *Acetaria* in 1699 wrote that Tarragon was, 'highly cordial and friendly to the head, heart and liver'.

Tarragon has its uses as a culinary herb, and the chopped dried or fresh leaves are excellent as a flavouring for cooked meat, fish and egg dishes and are especially good with chicken. Tarragon vinegar is also very popular.

Tobacco *(Nicotiana tabacum)*

There are at least 70 different species of Tobacco in the genus *Nicotiana*, which is part of the *Solanaceae* or Nightshade family. The mostly widely cultivated type is *N. tabacum*, and this is the species that is harvested for commercially available tobacco that is used to make cigarettes, cigars, pipe and rolling tobacco, and snuff. Because of the herb's most well-known use as a material for smoking with its potential risks to the health of smokers and its fiery nature, it is not surprising to find that Tobacco is ruled by the planet Mars.

Tobacco is regarded as a narcotic, a sedative and an emetic. It contains the poisonous alkaloid nicotine, which can be used as an insecticide. It is an addictive drug, which is why so many billions of people have become hooked as smokers. Wild forms of Tobacco, in particular *N. rustica* are even more potent as drugs and have been used by the shamans of some tribes as entheogens that help transport them to altered states. Sixteenth century physician Nicolas Monardes described a South American Indian's use of the herb when attempting to divine the cause of a patient's illness. After inhaling the Tobacco smoke, the shaman:

...fell downe upon the grounde, as a dedde manne, and remainyng so, according to the quantitie of the smoke that he had taken, and when the hearbe hath doen his woorke, he did revive and awake, and gave theim their answeres, accordyng to the visions, and illusions whiche he sawe.

Shamans from the Orinoco River area have been described as smoking five or six massive 1 metre cigars one after another to enter a trance state. This is a far cry from the modern use of Tobacco in cigarettes.

N. tabacum reaches around 2 metres in height and has very large pale green leaves and yellow flowers. *N. glauca* is known as the Tree Tobacco, and as its name suggest it reaches the size of a small tree. It has become an invasive weed in many subtropical and tropical parts of the world it has colonised, spreading along roadways and springing up on waste ground. The Navajo tribe used this plant in Peyote ceremonies and in other rituals. Tree Tobacco does not contain nicotine, but instead has an alkaloid known as anabasine, which also can be used as an insecticide.

Author Richard Rudgley, in his book *The Encyclopedia of Psychoactive Substances*, suggests that Tobacco was one of the earliest plants ever cultivated as a crop by tribal people in the distant past. He points out that these people had an ample supply of food sources all around so had no need to become farmers and yet the evidence shows that they grew Tobacco. Rudgley says that the Haida Indians of the Queen Charlotte Islands, off the West Coast of Canada, and the Tlingit from the south of Alaska, are examples of tribal peoples who cultivated Tobacco.

Wormwood *(Artemesia absinthium)*

Wormwood is another of the Artemesia family that is ruled by Mars, just like Tarragon, which has already been described. It is also known as 'Green Ginger', referring to its fiery nature. It is a very aromatic plant that is known for its exceeding bitterness. In the Bible, King Solomon describes the 'end of a strange woman' as being as 'bitter as Wormwood'.

It has been used medicinally though for a number of purposes and has been regarded as a useful herb since the ancient past. A 15th century manuscript states: 'Water of wormwood is gode – Grete Lords among the Saracens used to drinke hitt.'

It is a perennial plant that grows to around 1 metre in height. It has silvery-grey downy leaves that are finely cut and give off a strong aroma if bruised. The flowers are very small and a yellowish colour. It grows on waste ground, roadsides and river banks and comes from Europe, North and South America, Asia and South Africa. Wormwood is also often cultivated in herb gardens around the world.

The main use that Wormwood has been employed for is, as its name suggests, as an herbal cure for parasitic worms. It has actually become part of Dr Hulda Clark's controversial cancer cure and parasite removal programme. She says that cancers are caused by the human liver fluke along with other internal parasites and Wormwood is the main herb she prescribes to rid the body of these harmful invaders.

Wormwood has also been used as a remedy for jaundice, lack of appetite, as a tonic for the digestion, as a stimulant and as a treatment for epilepsy. Wormwood contains thujone, a substance that binds to the same brain receptors as THC from cannabis, and this is why it is thought to have psychoactive properties. There are American Indian tribes that smoke related species of *Artemesia*. Wormwood's potential mind-altering effects are thought to be why the alcoholic drink absinthe is so powerful.

Many famous artists and poets drank absinthe and it is thought to have helped inspire them creatively. Absinthe drinking could also cause brain damage, paralysis and blindness and was banned due to its harmful effects. Various, less powerful, versions of the drink are available today and it is often marketed as the 'Green Fairy'.

Despite its use as an ingredient in such a strong alcoholic drink, Wormwood has also been used to prevent drunkenness. Culpeper wrote that when the god Saturn happened upon Venus, the goddess of love, he found her as 'drunk as a hog' and this caused him to declare: 'What, thou a fortune and be drunk? I'll give thee antipathetical cure. Take my herb Wormwood and thou shalt never get a sufiet by drinking.'

Wormwood was once used as a strewing herb and to ward off insect pests such as flies and fleas. In magic it is regarded as a herb that can banish negativity. *A. canarienis*, a related species found in the Canary Islands, is called 'Incienso' in Spanish, referring to its strong aromatic properties, and a smell like incense.

Wormwood is also linked with the deities Aesculapius, Diana, Horus, Isis, and Castor and Pollux the Twins.

Herbs of Jupiter

Thorn
apple
datura
stramonium

Jupiter is the largest planet in our Solar System. It is composed of gases and has a very powerful magnetic field. Jupiter's keyword is expansion and it is associated with knowledge and philosophy, religion and speculative thought. Jupiter is also linked with the liver and the pituitary gland in the human body.

Agrimony (*Agrimonia eupatoria*)

Agrimony is a fairly common perennial plant of hedge-banks, grassy places and woodlands. It has compound leaves with many leaflets, is covered in downy hairs and has spikes of tiny apricot-scented yellow flowers in late summer. It is a member of the *Rosaceae*, so is a very distant relation to the Rose. It grows to around 60 centimetres in height and comes from the UK, Europe, Asia and North America. Agrimony should not be confused with the much-larger and unrelated Hemp Agrimony (*Eupatorium cannabinum*), which has pink flowers and grows to around 1.5 metres. Agrimony is ruled by Jupiter because in herbal medicine it is used as a treatment for liver diseases.

The scientific species name *eupatoria* is from Mithradates

Eupator, King of Pontus, who died long ago in 64 BC. It is said that he was a great believer in magical potions and also that he rendered himself immune to injury by saturating his body with lethal poisons. The Anglo-Saxons believed that Agrimony had magical powers and included the herb in their charms. A sprig of the plant placed under a pillow was said to bring oblivion until it was taken away. Agrimony was credited with the power to cure snake bites and charm away warts. It became the main herbal ingredient in 'eau d'arquebusade', a lotion that had the power to heal wounds inflicted by the 'arquebus', which was a 16th century firearm.

In herbal medicine, Agrimony is used to treat catarrh, sore throats, diarrhoea, cystitis and urinary infections, as well as being recommended as a remedy for liver, kidney and gall-bladder complaints. It has anti-inflammatory, antibacterial and astringent properties and the whole herb is gathered and made into infusions. It can also be used externally to help heal wounds. Agrimony, which yields a yellow dye from its flowers, is also known as 'Church Steeples'.

Lime Tree/Small-leaved Lime *(Tilia cordata)*

The Lime Tree is a very commonly planted tree from Europe and western Asia that is grown in parks and gardens and used to line streets. It is a native of some parts of the north of England. It is deciduous and grows as high as 38 metres. There are also the related species *T. Platyphyllos*, the Large-leaved Lime and *T. Americana*, the American Lime, as well as a hybrid known as *T. x europea* or the Common Lime. They are all very similar in appearance and in their medicinal properties. Limes have heart-shaped leaves and five-petal yellowish flowers that are carried in winged clusters and are highly perfumed. They are collected and dried for use and are also known as 'Linden Flowers'. The trees bloom in June and July and the air all around them becomes noticeably perfumed, attracting many bees. This is possibly why the Lime Tree is included in the herbs ruled by Jupiter, because filling the air with its scent like this is certainly expansive in nature.

In France, especially, a herbal tea known as 'Tilleul' is made from the flowers of the Lime. In Spain it is called 'Tila'. Lime flower tea has soothing properties and helps lower blood pressure. It increases perspiration and is good for treating colds, catarrh and fevers, as well as for anxiety and insomnia. Linden flower tea is often sweetened with honey.

It was once thought that Lime flowers were a remedy for epilepsy, or the 'Falling sickness' as it was known then. These ancient herbalists were certainly very optimistic though because they believed that an epileptic could be cured by merely sitting in the shade of the tree.

Richard Mabey in his classic book on foraging, *Food for Free*, informs us that the young leaves of the Lime are edible and can be eaten fresh or in sandwiches. The author describes them as 'thick, cooling and very glutinous'.

Meadowsweet *(Filipendula ulmaria)*

Meadowsweet is a very pretty wild flower that comes from Europe and Asia, but has been naturalised in America. It is known also known as 'Queen of the Meadows' and poet Ben Jonson called it 'meadow's queen' in his work. It is said to have been the favourite strewing herb of Queen Elizabeth I. Meadowsweet, as its name suggests, gives off a sweet perfume that can fill the air and it is this quality perhaps that makes the plant considered as a herb of Jupiter.

Meadowsweet tends to grow along river and stream banks, by ponds, in marshes and damp places in fields. It grows from a spreading rootstock, which could also be considered a quality of Jupiter, and reaches around 1 metre in height when in flower. It has aromatic pinnate leaves and the creamy white and frothy-looking flowers are carried in corymbs that are produced in summer.

The leaves and flowers are gathered for use in herbal medicine, and taken as an infusion it is considered a remedy for heartburn, stomach acidity and gastric ulcers. It has also been used to treat arthritis, rheumatism and urinary infections. Meadowsweet contains salicylic acid, which gives it anti-inflammatory and analgesic properties. The flowers when dried can be added to pot-pourri to which they add their strong scent. Fresh ones can be used to add flavouring to wines.

Meadowsweet is a sacred herb of the Druids. It was one of the flowers used to create Blodeuwedd, the 'Flower-faced' maiden, who was made by the magicians Math and Gwydion in the Welsh mythological story in the *Mabinogion*. 'Blodeu' is the Welsh for flowers and 'Gwedd' is a face. Blodeuwedd was made to be the wife of Lleu Llaw Gyffes, the hero of the story. The magicians took:

> ...the flowers of the oak, and the flowers of the broom, and the flowers of the meadowsweet, and from those they conjured up the fairest and most beautiful maiden anyone had ever seen. And they baptised her in the way that they did at that time, and named her Blodeuwedd.

Later on in the folktale, Blodeuwedd is cursed and transformed into an owl, and to this day, the name in Welsh signifies this nocturnal bird.

Oak (*Quercus robur*)

The Oak is a tree that is sacred to the Druids and has many magical and symbolic associations connected with it. It is ruled by Jupiter, and this is not surprising when you consider the vast expansiveness of its branches. It is the tree that the Druids harvest Mistletoe from at the time of Winter Solstice. Because this parasitic plant so rarely is found on Oak made it even more magical when it was discovered on this tree. Pliny the Elder, writing in the 1st century AD described the ceremony in this way:

> Hailing the moon in a native word that means 'healing all things', they prepare a ritual sacrifice and banquet beneath a tree and bring up two white bulls, whose horns are bound for the first time on this occasion. A priest arrayed in white vestments climbs the tree and, with a golden sickle, cuts down the mistletoe, which is caught in a white cloak. Then finally they kill the victims, praying to a god to render his gift propitious to those on whom he has bestowed it. They believe that mistletoe given in drink will impart fertility to any animal that is barren and that it is an antidote to all poisons.

Philip Carr-Gomm, a leader of the Order of Bards, Ovates and Druids OBOD), writing in *The Elements of the Druid Tradition*, of the derivation of the word Druid, stated:

> Not all scholars are able to agree about its etymology, but most modern authorities agree with the classical authors that the most likely derivation is from the word for oak, combined with the Indo-European root 'wid' – to know, giving their translation of the word Druid as 'One with knowledge of the oak' or 'Wise man of the oak'.

There is a lot of evidence in support of this idea because 'Derw' is the Welsh for Oak and 'Derwydd' means a Druid. In Irish 'Daur' is an Oak and 'Drui' is the word for Druid.

A strongly held pagan and Wiccan belief that is celebrated each year is the ongoing power struggle between the Oak King and the Holly King, in which the Oak King rules the land from Midwinter to Midsummer when he is replaced by the Holly King, who is in command for the second half of the Wheel of the Year.

The Common Oak or English Oak is a native of the UK and much of Europe. The American species, known as the White Oak (*Q. alba*) also has a history of use in herbal medicine just like its European cousin.

Among the superstitions and customs that surround the Oak is the belief that the tree can offer protection from lightning, and so it is a good idea to plant it in the vicinity of buildings. Carrying an acorn was thought to preserve youth, while the dew collected from under this tree was an important ingredient in beauty potions and lotions. In 1969, former Beatle John Lennon, together with his wife Yoko Ono, started a campaign in which participants were asked to plant an acorn for peace.

Oak bark is the part that is gathered for use in herbal medicine. It has astringent, anti-inflammatory and antiseptic properties and is believed to be good for controlling bleeding. Oak is applied externally to cuts and abrasions, skin irritations, ulcers, varicose veins and haemorrhoids. Young Oak leaves can be used as the basis for a home-made wine.

Pine *(Pinus species)*

Pines are ruled by Jupiter just like several other trees. This is presumably because of how their branches can fan out covering a lot of space and pine forests can do likewise with the ground they cover. The Scots Pine (*P. sylvestris*) is the species listed in most books about herbs. This tree comes from Europe, Turkey and Asia, as well as Scotland in the UK, as its name suggests. Like most pine trees, it bears pine needles in the place of leaves and pine cones as its fruits. This coniferous tree can reach 40 metres in height and is often found growing wild on moors and mountainsides, as well as being widely cultivated for its ornamental value in parks and large gardens.

In Celtic treelore the Scots Pine is included in what is known as the Beth-Luis-Nion Tree Calendar and Alphabet. It is known as the 'Ailm' and represents the A vowel, and its date in the seasonal calendar is 22 December or the time of the Winter Solstice. The pine cone is a symbol of male fertility because of the many seeds it contains. The cone is carried by the deities Dionysus and Bacchus. It forms the tip of their wands, which are bound with evergreen Ivy. It is also connected with the pineal gland, thought to be the 'third eye', the seat of psychic illumination in the human body, and said to resemble a very tiny pine cone. This could be another reason why the Pine is regarded as a herb of Jupiter. The Scots Pine is sacred to Artemis and Druantia, the Gallic Fir Goddess, who is thought of as the 'Keeper of the Sacred Grove' and the 'Fountain of Renewal'.

Pines contain aromatic resin with pinene as an active constituent. Essential oil of pine can be used as an inhalant and as a treatment for respiratory complaints. Pine needle herbal tea has tonic properties and the distilled pine oil is used in perfumes and soaps. A handful of pine shoots added to bathwater will help relive rheumatic aches and pains. Pine nuts are edible.

The Maritime Pine (*P. maritima/pinaster*) has been found to be an excellent source of pycnogenol, a very powerful antioxidant that has been widely sold by health stores and suppliers of herbal and mineral supplements. Pycnogenol is used to protect against free-radical damage and strengthen the immune system.

Sassafras *(Sassafras albidum)*
Sassafras is an aromatic deciduous tree that is native to North America and some southern parts of Canada, and is ruled, like several other trees, by Jupiter. It has oval, two-lobed and three-lobed leaves, reddish-brown bark and reaches 6 metres or more in height. The flowers are small and greenish-yellow and are carried in clusters in April and May. They are followed by dark-blue berries. The tree's name is thought to be a corruption of the Spanish for 'Saxifrage', and was first used by the botanist Nicolas Monardes in the 16th century. It is reported that Sir Francis Drake first brought Sassafras into Britain, and also that

the Spanish went on to use it in pomanders in an effort to repel the plague that was killing so many people.

Sassafras tea has been made from the root-bark, though in 1976 the FDA banned safrole, a major constituent, due to its carcinogenic properties. Before this the tea was very popular and could even be bought in London. It is also known as 'saloop'. Sassafras leaves do not have enough of this substance in them to be affected by the ruling. In cooking, the leaves of Sassafras have been used in Louisiana to flavour soups, stews and sauces. It is the main spice in the Cajun dish known as 'Gumbo filé'.

Sassafras has stimulant and diuretic properties, and has been used in herbal medicine to treat colds and fevers, as well as a remedy for gout and rheumatism. However, because the tree has been considered to be carcinogenic and due to the FDA ban on safrole, it has fallen out of favour with some practitioners.

Sassafras is believed to have magical properties, and is said to be useful if you want to attract money. To do this the herb is placed in a wallet or purse, or alternatively added to incense and burned as part of a spell to gain wealth.

Thorn Apple (*Datura stramonium*)

The Thorn Apple, or 'Devil's Weed', as it is also known, is a poisonous herb from the *Solanaceae* or Nightshade family. It is an annual and grows on rough ground, waste places, roadsides and cultivated soil in many parts of the world, though is thought to have originated in the southern parts of North America, and from Central and South America, as well as Asia. Thorn Apple grows to 1 metre or more in height and has large jagged leaves, white or purple-tinged funnel-shaped flowers and spiky seed-pods that give the plant one of its names. It gives off an offensive smell if lightly brushed against, although the flowers are scented. The thick stems branch out and are either green or a purplish colour. The prickly fruits contain hundreds of small dark kidney-bean-shaped seeds.

Thorn Apple is ruled by Jupiter possibly because of its expansive qualities. The plant distributes itself across patches of ground very readily by self-seeding. If consumed internally, Thorn Apple is a very dangerous hallucinogen that can cause visions of other places in a vastly altered reality. An individual intoxicated by this herb may experience seeing people they know or being in familiar locations. It creates a dream world that is experienced as being as real as this world. This ability to move a person affected by the alkaloid drugs in Thorn Apple out of where their physical body, so that they believe themselves to be elsewhere, is another quality of Jupiter. Thorn Apple was an ingredient in flying ointments used by witches. It contains the dangerous substances atropine and hyoscyamine and scopolamine.

European settlers in America had discovered the narcotic properties of the plant and it became known as 'Jimson Weed', after it was collected by soldiers in the Jamestown area in 1676. It is said that the men mistook it for edible greens with disastrous consequences because they became incoherent for 11 days afterwards and were in no state to deal with the Jamestown Riots. 'Jimson' is, of course, a corruption of Jamestown. In 38 BC, a similar incident happened when Mark Anthony's troops made the same mistake and ate the plant after cooking it.

Many Native American tribes have used the herb in initiation ceremonies. In India it is mentioned in Vedic literature and is an herb that is sacred to Lord Shiva, the Hindu god of death and destruction. The ancient Greeks used it as an herb employed as an oracle, while the Chinese considered it as usable as an anaesthetic.

Thorn Apple has been used in herbal medicine as a treatment for asthma, neuralgia and against Parkinson's disease, but it is far too toxic and should never be considered as safe for domestic purposes. As well as hallucinations and disorientation, Thorn Apple produces dryness of the mouth, dizziness, slurred speech and a state like extreme drunkenness, as well as amnesia after it has worn off. It can cause coma, convulsions and permanent damage to the heart, brain and vision.

Nevertheless, despite the obvious dangers the herb can cause, it became of interest to recreational drug-users after the plant was publicised in Hunter S. Thompson's *Fear and Loathing in Las Vegas* and in Carlos Castaneda's *The Teaching's of Don Juan*, where it is included as a 'power plant' used by the Yaqui Indian sorcerers. Castaneda writes that after an ointment containing Datura was rubbed into his leg:

> I looked down and saw Don Juan sitting below me... I saw the dark sky above me and the clouds going by me. I jerked my body so I could look down. I saw the dark mass of the mountains.

This suggests that he was flying or astral travelling.

Besides its associations with the Devil; in Spanish it is known as Hierba del Diablo ('Herb of the Devil'), the Thorn Apple is also linked with the Angel Gabriel.

Herbs of Saturn

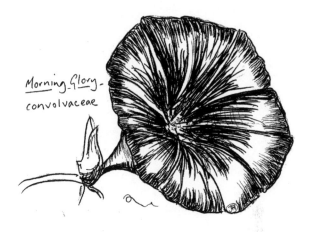

Morning Glory - convolvaceae

Saturn was once regarded as the outermost planet in the solar system, and because of this limitation became its keyword. It was at the very limits known. Saturn is associated with several parts of the body, including the skin, teeth, bones, gall-bladder and spleen. It is also linked with old age, tenacity, restriction and perseverance. Saturn is well-known for being circled by its rings, which were not able to be seen with the naked eye because the planet was so far away from Earth.

Deadly Nightshade (*Atropa belladonna*)

Deadly Nightshade is, as its name suggests, a very poisonous plant. Like the Thorn Apple, Henbane and Mandrake it is a member of the *Solanaceae* and like them it carries a number of hallucinogenic, but dangerous, tropane alkaloids in it including atropine and scopolamine. It is a perennial shrub that forms bushes that reach as much as 1.5 metres in height, and grows in woods, thickets, hedges and waste places in the UK, Europe, Asia and North America, especially on chalky soils. Deadly Nightshade has dull-green ovate leaves and bell-shaped purplish-brown flowers that are followed by black berries. These berries are very poisonous and are also known as 'Devil's berries', 'Devil's Cherries', 'Naughty Man's Cherries', 'Sorcerer's Cherry' and 'Witch's Berry'.

Deadly Nightshade has many links with witchcraft and was used in flying ointments, as well as in various spells and potions. It is not surprisingly connected with the darker side of magic and has a very real power over life and death. This is why it is ruled by Saturn. The scientific name *Atropa* is derived from Atropos, who was one of the Fates in Greek mythology, a supernatural being credited with carrying the shears that could cut the thread of human life. Deadly Nightshade is also, not surprisingly, linked with the dark Goddess Hecate.

Legends tell that the Devil himself tends to the Deadly Nightshade as a favourite herb, and the only night he can be guaranteed to be not looking after it is Walpurgis Night, when he is too busy getting ready for the witches' Sabbath. Ancient British priests are said to have drunk a dangerous and potent infusion of Deadly Nightshade before invoking Bellona, the goddess of war. Bellona is very similar to *belladonna*, which may be a corruption of this, or more like comes from the two words 'bella' and 'donna' that translate as 'beautiful lady' in Italian. The juice of Deadly Nightshade is known to dilate the pupils of the eye and was once used for this purpose by women who sought to make themselves look seductive.

It has been used in ophthalmic diagnosis and surgery because of this effect it has on the eyes. Deadly Nightshade has had other medicinal uses too, including being employed in the treatment of blood pressure, asthma, stomach ulcers, spasms and hyper-acidity, as well as in homeopathy. Because of the very real danger of poisoning from this herb, though, it must be stressed that its use is never for domestic purposes.

Deadly Nightshade poisoning causes dry mouth, flushed skin, vomiting, lack of coordination, delirium, convulsions and breathing failure leading to death. Survivors may well have sustained permanent damage to their brains and eyesight. In cases of poisoning it is recommended that the victim is given something, such as warm vinegar or mustard, to make them sick. Otherwise, a stomach pump is likely to be used, followed by magnesia and a stimulant such as strong coffee. As a matter of interest, horses, sheep, goats, rabbits and pigs are all reported as more or less immune to the toxic properties of Deadly Nightshade, although cats and dogs are poisoned just like humans. Buchanan wrote in the *History of Scotland* (1582) of the tradition that claimed that at the time of King Duncan I's reign Macbeth's soldiers poisoned an entire army of Danish invaders by mixing Deadly Nightshade into the wine they were served.

Hemlock *(Conium maculatum)*

Hemlock is another very poisonous herb ruled by Saturn, presumably because it has the power of causing death. It is a tall biennial plant that can grow to around 2 metres in height and is found on waste ground, on roadsides and riverbanks in parts of the UK, Europe, Asia and North Africa, as well as in America where it was introduced. Hemlock is in the *Apiaceae* or Parsley family, and like so many others in this plant group, it bears umbels of small white flowers. It also has feathery and fernlike foliage and could easily be mistaken for a harmless species in this family, although fortunately Hemlock has two signs that help to clearly identify it. The stems are peppered with dark purplish spots and the whole plant gives off a most unpleasant smell.

Hemlock has a narcotic and sedative action that produces paralysis and then death. The name *Conium* is thought to have been derived from the Greek 'kona' that means to be whirling about, such as someone experiencing vertigo would suffer. This is a condition Hemlock poisoning could produce, but it is also said that, horrific as the symptoms are, the mind stays alert right until the last moments. Hemlock was used as a method of execution in ancient Greece, while in Rome it was mixed with opium and was taken as a means of suicide. The philosopher Socrates is probably the most famous historical figure to have been killed by drinking the juice of Hemlock.

Hemlock has had some uses in herbal medicine though and was employed as an antidote to strychnine poisoning. It was thought that the one poison would cancel out the effect of the other. Also it was once employed as a treatment for whooping cough, epilepsy and other illnesses in which there are spasms and seizures. Obviously due to its very toxic nature, caused by the alkaloid coniine, Hemlock should never be used now. In Medieval times, however, Hemlock was mixed with Betony (*Betonica officinalis*) and the seed of Fennel and prescribed as a remedy for the bite of a rabid dog. The herbalist Culpeper claimed that Hemlock stopped all 'lustful thoughts' although it is more likely that it stopped all thoughts!

Not surprisingly Hemlock has found its uses in witchcraft and the dark side of the occult and has been associated with death. Hemlock like Deadly Nightshade is also linked with the goddess Hecate. It was one of the herbs used in flying ointments, and there are grimoires that suggested that a ritual dagger used by a magician for casting a circle should be first dipped in a mixture of the blood of a black cat and Hemlock juice.

Hemlock is also known as 'Bad Man's Oatmeal', 'Beaver Poison', 'Hecklow', 'Hylic', 'Kex' and 'Poison Parsley'.

Henbane (*Hyoscamus niger*)

Henbane is yet another very poisonous herb ruled by Saturn as well as being yet another plant from the Nightshade family. An annual or biennial it grows to as much as 1 metre in height in optimum conditions, but is often a lot smaller. Henbane is usually found by the sea and on sandy waste ground. It has grey-green sticky leaves that give off an unpleasant smell and bell-shaped creamy-yellow flowers delicately veined with purple. The flowers are followed by seed-pods that form capsules like little pots along the stems that are full of seeds. Henbane comes from the Mediterranean, but is also found in the UK, Europe and Asia.

Henbane contains the dangerous tropane alkaloids hyoscyamine, scopolamine and atropine, also found in Deadly Nightshade and Thorn Apple. It produces hallucinations and delirium. Intoxication with Henbane can easily result in death though, which is one of its Saturnine qualities. It has been used medicinally, however, as a treatment for asthma and as a remedy for spasms. The herbalist Joseph Miller reported that: 'The roots are frequently hung about children's necks...to prevent fits and cause an easy breeding of the teeth.'

Gerard wrote:

The seed is used by mountebank tooth-drawers which run about the country, to cause worms to come forth of the teeth by burning it in a chafing dish of coles, the party holding his mouth over the fume thereof; but some crafty companions to gain money convey small lute-strings into the water persuading the patient that these small creepers came out of his mouth or other part which he intended to ease.

He also stated: 'To wash the feet in a decoction of Henbane causeth sleep, or given in a clyster it doth the same, and also the often smelling to the flowers.'

The scientific name *hyoscyamus* means 'bean of the hog' and it is said that pigs are immune to the poisons in this plant. Culpeper decided it was an herb of Saturn, apparently because he thought it was found in Saturnine locations. He wrote: 'Whole cartloads of it may be found near the places where they empty the common Jakes and scarce a ditch is found without the growing of it.'

Henbane was used in the flying ointments and magical brews of the medieval witches, and paste of the herb was used as a poison after being smeared on arrows of the ancient Celts. It was also known to the ancient Egyptians, Greeks and Romans.

Henbane is also known as 'Belene', 'Caniculata', 'Cassilata', 'Devil's Eye', 'Hebenon', 'Isana', 'Poison Tobacco', 'Stinking Roger', 'Symphonica' and 'Tooth-wort'. Whatever you choose to call it, it goes without saying that Henbane is far too dangerous as a herb to be used for domestic purposes. Like many other herbs of Saturn, it has the power of causing death.

Monkshood (Aconitum napellus)

Monkshood or Aconite is yet another very poisonous plant that is ruled by Saturn. In fact, it is one of the most toxic plants in the world and just a small amount can produce numbness, vomiting, coma and death. Just touching the plant can cause allergic reactions too and it really is a 'femme fatale' of the plant kingdoms. Monkshood is an herb in which you can admire its beauty, but it is best left alone. The whole plant is very toxic and gloves should be worn if you do need to handle it.

Monkshood is a hardy perennial that can reach 1.5 metres in height. It is found growing wild on riverbanks and in damp woodlands in the UK and many parts of Europe and is also cultivated as a garden flower. It has delphinium-like divided foliage and tuberous roots. Its scientific name Napellus actually means a 'little turnip', but this description gives no indication of the poisonous nature of the Monkshood roots. It takes its English moniker from its flowers that are helmet-shaped and an inky purple-blue colour.

The closely related and very similar looking, though it has yellow flowers, A. lycotonum is known as Wolf's Bane, and was once used for killing these animals. Referring to Monkshood's poisonous nature the herbalist Gerard wrote of a 'lamentable experiment' in which some 'ignorant persons' from Antwerp sickened and died after mistaking the plant for greens that could be eaten in salad.

Other names for Monkshood include 'Chariot of Venus', 'Dumbledore's Delight', 'Friar's Cowl', 'Helmet Flower', 'Queen Mother of Poisons', and 'Storm Hat'. As a poison it was used to kill Pope Adrian VI, and there was an assassination plot against Alexander the Great using it too. In Greek myth the enchantress Medea was said to have poisoned the cup of the hero Theseus with this deadly plant.

Nevertheless, despite its dangers, Monkshood has also been used medicinally in the past as a sedative and painkiller, and also it is employed in homeopathy. Obviously this is a herb not to be used for domestic purposes apart from perhaps growing it in your herb garden.

Monkshood is associated with the goddess Hecate and with Cerberus of the Underworld. In witchcraft it has been used as an ingredient of flying ointments like many other very toxic herbs.

Morning Glory *(Ipomoea violacea)*

Morning Glory is the name of several species of vine in the Bindweed family or *Convolvulaceae*. They all have funnel-shaped flowers and grow as climbers. The Morning Glories come from Central America and the southern States of North America, but many are grown worldwide as garden plants because of their colourful flowers and fast-growing vines that can be trained up fences or trellises or used to cover walls.

The most well-known species of Morning Glory is *I. violacea* or *tricolor*. It comes in many different colour variations including 'Heavenly Blue', the creamy white 'Pearly Gates' and the blue and white 'Flying Saucers' and has heart-shaped leaves. These very 'cosmic' sounding names are very apt because this species of Morning Glory contains lysergic acid amide (LSA) and can produce a psychedelic experience if consumed. This, of course, led the plant to be popular with hippies and 'psychonauts' looking for 'legal' entheogens to take for mind-expanding trips.

One seed contains the equivalent of around one microgram of

LSD. The seeds have to be soaked in water or ground up into powder. They tend to produce physical sickness due to chemicals in them so are in no way as popular as 'acid'. The hallucinogenic experience the seeds provide is also a lot milder in intensity.

Morning Glory seeds have a long history of use by the shamans of the tribal people of Central America and Mexico. The Aztecs, Mayans, Mazatecs, Mixe and Zapotecs are some of the tribes that have used Morning Glory to help them reach other realities and to communicate with the spirit worlds.

The mind-expanding properties of the Morning Glory have earned it a place in the herbs of Saturn, although it is also connected with the Virgin Mary and all mother goddesses.

Patchouli (Pogostemon cablin)
Patchouli or Patchouly, as it is also spelled, is a very aromatic tropical herb from the Labiate or Mint and Sage family. A very strong and heady perfume is made from the plant and this became very popular with the hippie movement in the 1960s and 1970s. It became associated with the Far East where alternative religious paths were to be found along with gurus and meditation. Patchouli is a well-known ingredient for incense and in aromatic oils. It is linked with the mind-expanding and contemplative practices that so many people turned to in that era and in Asia, and for this reason it is a herb of Saturn.

Patchouli grows to between 60 and 90 centimetres in height and bears purplish-pink-white flowers that turn into small dark seeds. It is a bushy plant that comes originally from parts of tropical Asia but is now widely cultivated in China, India, Indonesia, Malaysia, The Philippines, Taiwan, Thailand, Vietnam, and also in West Africa. There are several similar species related to P. cablin with similar properties, and all of which are also cultivated.

The leaves of Patchouli are harvested and the oil is processed by distillation. Patchouli oil finds its way into many products where perfumes are used. Patchouli has had medicinal uses too and it has been employed as a remedy for snake-bite in Malaysia and Japan. In Chinese medicine it is used to treat headaches, colds and digestive disorders. The scent of Patchouli is an aid to relaxation and the oil is used in aromatherapy. Patchouli has also found a use as an insecticide.

Skullcap *(Scutellaria galericulata)*

Skullcap is in the same family as Patchouli because it is yet another herb in the *Labiatae,* and like Patchouli it is ruled by Saturn. It is a perennial plant that is found growing in marshes, along streams and in ditches. Skullcap comes from the UK, Europe and North America and reaches less than 1 metre in height. It has purplish-blue flowers that look like little helmets and have given it the names 'Helmet Flower' and 'Hoodwort'.

Skullcap is used in herbal medicine to treat insomnia and nervous disorders, but can produce giddiness if too much is taken. It has tranquillising and sedative properties and is also anti-inflammatory in its action. Skullcap has been used as a treatment for malaria and even to combat rabies. It has the alternative names of 'Mad-dog Skullcap' and 'Madweed'. When smoked it is said to have an effect a bit like marijuana.

Skullcap was believed to be a cure for infertility, and if worn by women it was thought that this would stop their husbands from committing adultery and going off with other women.

Bibliography

Andrews, Steve and Katrinia Rindsberg, *Herbs of the Northern Shaman*, O-Books, Winchester UK, Washington USA, 2010

Bleakley, Alan, *Fruits of the Moon Tree*, Gateway Books, Bath, 1991

Castaneda, Carlos, *The Teachings of Don Juan*, Simon & Schuster, Pocket Books, New York, 1974

Culpeper, N., *The English Physician and Complete Herbal*, Lewis and Roden, London, 1805

Gerard, J., *The Herball or Generall Historie of Plantes*, John Norton, London, 1597

Grieve F.R.H.S, Mrs M., *A Modern Herbal*, Tiger Books, London, 1992

Houdret, Jessica, *The Ultimate Book of Herbs & Herb Gardening*, Hermes House, London, 2002

Launett, Edmund, *The Hamlyn Guide to Edible and Medicinal Plants of Britain and Northern Europe*, Hamlyn, London, 1981

Lavender, Susan and Anna Franklin, *Herb Craft*, Capall Bann, Berks, UK, 1996

Mabey, Richard, *Food For Free*, Collins, London, 1972

Parker, Derek and Julia, *The Compleat Astrologer*, Mitchell Beazley, London, 1979

Podlech, Dieter, *Collins Nature Guide: Herbs and Healing Plants of Britain and Europe*, UK Edition, Harper Collins, London, 1996

Potterton, David, *Culpeper's Colour Herbal*, W. Foulsham & Company, London, 1983

Rudgley, Richard, *The Encyclopaedia of Psychoactive Substances*, Little, Brown and Company, London, 1998

Index